Film/Fiction volume 2

Trash Aesthetics

Popular Culture and Its Audience

Edited by
**Deborah Cartmell, I.Q. Hunter, Heidi Kaye
and Imelda Whelehan**

Pluto  Press

LONDON • STERLING, VIRGINIA

First published 1997 by Pluto Press
345 Archway Road, London N6 5AA
and 22883 Quicksilver Drive, Sterling
VA 20166–2012, USA

British Library Cataloguing in Publication Data
A catalogue record for this book is available from the British
Library

ISBN 0 7453 1203 9 hbk

Library of Congress Cataloging in Publication Data
Trash aesthetics: popular culture and its audience/edited by
    Deborah Cartmell ... [et al.].
        p.   cm. — (Film/fiction: v. 2)
    Includes bibliographical references and index.
    ISBN 0–7453–1203–9
    1. Motion pictures—Aesthetics. 2. Popular culture.
    I. Cartmell, Deborah. II. Series.
    PN1995.T64   1997
    791.43'01—dc21   96–45671
                                                          CIP

03   02   01   00   99   98
6   5   4   3   2

Designed and produced for Pluto Press by
Chase Production Services, Chadlington, OX7 3LN
Typeset from disk by Stanford DTP Services, Milton Keynes
Printed in the EC

Trash Aesthetics

2

R

Film/Fiction

The Film/Fiction series addresses the developing interface between English and Media studies, in particular the cross-fertilisation of methods and debates applied to analyses of literature, film and popular culture. Not only will this series capitalise upon growing links between departments of English and Media throughout Britain, it will also debate the consequences of the blurring of such disciplinary boundaries.

Editors
Deborah Cartmell – I.Q. Hunter – Heidi Kaye – Imelda Whelehan

Advisory Editor
Tim O'Sullivan

Also available
Deborah Cartmell, I.Q. Hunter, Heidi Kaye and Imelda Whelehan (eds)
Pulping Fictions: Consuming Culture Across the Literature/Media Divide

Future volumes will focus on Sisterhood, Aliens and the New Millennium. Anyone interested in proposing contributions to Film/Fiction should contact the editors at the Department of English, Media and Cultural Studies, School of Humanities, De Montfort University, Leicester, LE1 9BH, UK.

Contents

Introduction – Trash Aesthetics: Popular Culture and its Audience

I.Q. Hunter and Heidi Kaye

Postmodernism, it has been said, means never having to say you're sorry.[1] With the collapse of universally applicable standards of aesthetic judgement, postmodern audiences are supposedly free to make of texts pretty much what they like. No one, in this whirl of cultural relativism, need ever apologise for their pleasures.

Recent cultural criticism has explored more deeply than ever before the undergrowth of literature and popular film, shifting attention from what ideal audiences should be reading and viewing to what real people actually enjoy. As well as discovering unexpected complexity in 'trash culture', the result has been a heightened awareness of the differences between audiences, and of the importance of specialised constituencies such as fans and cultists. The most vibrant current research is committed to taking audiences and their pleasures seriously. Going beyond either castigating them for poor taste or worrying obsessively about the effects of popular culture, it asks instead what real, unruly, socially situated readers and viewers *do* with texts. Audiences are no longer envisaged as passive consumers but as active producers of popular culture.

The essays in *Trash Aesthetics*, the second volume in the *Film/Fiction* series, draw from this audience-centred approach to popular culture. Extending the work of such critics as Ien Ang, Camille Bacon-Smith, Michel de Certeau, Henry Jenkins and Constance Penley, they re-examine the role of popular audiences in breaking down boundaries between genres, media

1

forms and high and low culture. All of the texts discussed, from comics to exploitation films, have been appropriated, reinterpreted and otherwise enjoyed by distinct audiences, whether fans or academic critics.

The book's emphasis on despised forms reflects the convergence of English and Media studies in the 1980s and 1990s, and the hegemony of what has been called 'cultural populism'.[2] In the face of considerable journalistic and some academic antagonism, such approaches continue to validate the study (and even the celebration) of supposedly ephemeral and trivial products of popular culture. Press attacks on the 'softness' of Media studies in particular as a kind of *trahison des clercs* have proliferated over the last few years, which have seen a boom in student enrolment for the subject.[3] Haunted by visions of students preferring Tarantino to Shakespeare, Media studies' detractors fear both an accelerated Americanisation of British culture and a general lowering of standards of aesthetic value. Yet, popular culture is increasingly seen as diversified and demanding of its audience's intertextual literacy and interpretative activity. Growing numbers of adaptations of 'classic' literature, novelisations of films and new media such as laser disks, CD-ROMs and the Internet blur the lines between film and fiction, reader and author, spectator and participant as well as between mass and elite culture. Such a democratisation of culture is as threatening as the widening of access to higher education to the traditionalists in authority and the academy, so it is not surprising that the rapid growth and popularity of Media studies meets with such virulent abuse; nevertheless, it is a sign of a vibrant society.[4]

This more sympathetic interest in popular culture has come about partly because academics nowadays more frequently identify with popular audiences rather than disdainfully pathologise mass taste, and partly because cultural theory has shifted in practice towards a merger of post-structuralism and ethnography. It builds on post-structuralism's assertion that readers construct rather than simply receive meaning (which implies that even critical interpretations are imaginative confabulations)[5] by presenting case studies of specific audiences.

A key influence here is the sociologist Pierre Bourdieu, who argues in *Distinction*, his influential study of French bourgeois culture, that aesthetic judgements are neither natural nor disinterested but work as disguised methods of class distinction.[6] Listening to Wagner rather than Mantovani is, from this corrosively cynical point of view, much like preferring Volvos to Ford Escorts or Ralph Lauren to Marks and Spencer: it's a learned reflex, a skirmish in semiotic class warfare. Postmodern critics go even further in emphasising the differences between audiences, almost to the point of reviving methodological individualism; this kind of ethnographic description is closer in fact to market research than to conventional textual analysis. Interpretation and aesthetic judgement, they maintain, are also functions of one's gender, race and sexuality, indeed of every aspect of oneself that is caught up in relations of power. But they reject any simplistic model of audiences being manipulated by culture, focusing instead on the interactive relationship between heterogeneous, self-reflexive audiences and infinitely reinterpretable texts. Neither texts nor audiences are univocal; the meanings and pleasures of texts are rather defined by how they are appropriated by audiences to suit specific and often incommensurable needs. Academics are learning what advertising agencies have always known: the power of consumer sovereignty. Everyone is a potential niche market. One of the many pleasures of consumer capitalism is that it so perfectly services this fragmented, postmodern individual. Out there in the global pick 'n' mix is a text made just for you; or a text you can customise to your suit your desires. If you don't like techno, there's New Age; if you don't like the *Guardian*, there's *Sunday Sport*; if you don't like *Showgirls* (1995) (and, alas, not many did), there's always *Orlando* (1994).

We are urged, therefore, not to take aesthetic judgements for granted. We should understand them instead as forms of 'cultural capital', both exertions of social power and exercises in self-description. In spite of the apparent determinism of Bourdieu's approach, audiences are never wholly predictable, never just the playthings of hypnotically suggestive texts. This notion of the self-reflexive active audience obviously tends to undermine the more paranoid styles of political criticism, which rely on uncovering the dangerous ideological messages covertly transmitted in popular culture. Symptomatic interpretation remains a common approach to popular culture, encouraged by the popularity of psychoanalysis. One newspaper critic, for instance, was able to cobble together a symptomatic explanation for the hit alien-invasion movie *Independence Day* (1996), confidently asserting that the aliens were 'really' illegal Hispanic immigrants.[7] On some 'deep' level hidden to all but the critic, the aliens were transmogrified in the warped dream-life of the atavistic masses. Reading movies becomes a means of diagnosing (especially American) audiences as susceptible 'Others'.

As the contributors to *Trash Aesthetics* maintain, audiences in fact consist of numerous awkward individuals, whose interpretations and pleasures are complicated, informed and often downright weird. No one, for instance, could anticipate the serial killer Jeffrey Dahmer's fascination with *Return of the Jedi* (1983); identifying with the all-powerful Emperor, he obsessively watched the film over and over again, and even bought yellow contact lenses to look more like his hero;[8] or the fans of *Withnail and I* (1986), whose rituals include drinking along with the leading characters until they pass out; or the critic Barbara Creed's contention that the monster in *Alien* (1979) is the phallus of the archaic mother – a display of psychoanalytic cultural capital incomprehensible outside the academy.[9] An intriguing result of critical interest in cults and fans is to blur the seemingly obvious distinctions between such 'eccentric' (over)interpreters and 'sensible' readers, and between fans and academics. A key question raised in this book is therefore what claim to authority the academic reading has over the 'general' audience's, especially when critics are reconceived as just one more species of audience, or even as a particular type of fan.[10] Martin Barker, for instance, is concerned about the influence his status as academic researcher may have on his individual respondent's answers to his questionnaire. Roberta Pearson considers the ethics of her intervention in the Internet discussion groups on Sherlock Holmes. Helen Merrick questions critics' attachment to the idea that they are separate from the fan cultures they describe and discusses the problem of privileging 'expert' readings over those of the fans when the critic identifies herself as a fan as well.

We should ask, then, not only why mass audiences like certain texts, but why academic critics do as well. Why, for example, was it so blindingly obvious to critics everywhere that Paul Verhoeven's sex-film *Showgirls* was an obnoxiously bad movie? What was the source of this self-evident truth? More to the point, what about those in the audience, the lonely, despised, sadly misguided few, who admitted to liking the film? Were they mad, or ignorant or simply and uninterestingly wrong, as wrong as someone who is bored by *Citizen Kane* (1942) or finds a Big Mac incomparably delicious? Who in the end decides such matters? In fact, since its release, *Showgirls* has found a niche as a camp cult among gay New Yorkers, who perform along with the film at special screenings, calling out favourite lines and imitating the more energetic dance routines. They gleefully appropriate the film from its intended audience of overheated heterosexual males. But this camp resurrection (as Verhoeven described it), which embraces and celebrates the dominant response to the movie ('It's terrible!'), makes it even more difficult for 'genuine' fans to argue its merits with a straight face. One would have to reappropriate it from ironic admirers who were never meant to like it in the first place.

The obvious drawback of the post-structuralist/postmodern emphasis on audiences is that, with aesthetic judgements put on hold and audiences boldly reinvented as active generators of meaning and pleasure, few positive reasons are left to prefer one text to another. On the one hand, audiences seem firmly trapped in their likes and dislikes, which depend entirely on the particular fraction of the population to which they belong. On the other, they are postmodern free spirits, making it all up as they go along, ironising, appropriating and sub-creating to their hearts' content. For while audience-centred research usefully dispels the more dim-witted assumptions about the 'masses' – that they are stupid, passive, unreflective in consumption – it is of little help when it comes to choosing between or making sense of books and movies. For the politically sensitive critic, one means is to privilege the readings and preferences of the most 'resistant' or 'transgressive' audience. This desire to invest popular culture with subversive potential can lead to a romanticisation of certain audiences, while other, insufficiently marginal audiences (such as white, male fans of action movies) are ignored or demonised.

Even so, just because half-a-dozen teenagers in Lewisham read *Neighbours* transgressively, or, as Martin Barker describes in this volume, one Australian fascist finds Judge Dredd seductive, the rest of us surely feel no obligation to adjust our *own* readings and tastes accordingly. Equally, because our readings and tastes are apt to be smugly redescribed as socially determined ('Only a white yuppie would like that!'), it doesn't necessarily follow that they are any less 'right' for us – though we might, as good postmodernists, get more self-conscious and guiltily ironic about them. Here, as in other places (we leave the active reader to interpret where), the co-authors of this introduction divide, as individuals from different audience constituencies. Postmodern hedonism needs to be tempered by the recognition that while political correctness may well be anathema, political apathy is far worse, in criticism as elsewhere.

The meanings invested in texts, whether by authors, directors, fans or critics, have a political dimension, yet no single political interpretation is sufficient to cover the diversity of audience responses. Popular culture is engaged in a creative dialogue with its audiences, who choose or adapt texts to suit their outlooks. We need not only to ask why certain audiences respond to certain texts, but also to explore the implications of the contexts and products of those responses in our culture. Texts seem to demand the creation by the audience of yet more texts: fans writing stories for zines, cultists reinventing disregarded films, net surfers trading information on fictional worlds. The interactions within subcultures developed around different cultural forms, be they Trekkies or Jane Austen enthusiasts, are located in a variety of contexts, from face-to-face meetings at conventions or conferences, through fanzines and newsletters, to Usenet groups and websites. These different contexts offer a diverse range of 'interpretive communities', to use Stanley Fish's phrase, positions from which groups and individuals relate to each other and make meaning through texts.[11] The dynamics of these positions and the conditions which make them available to individuals have recently begun to come under study.

The book begins with studies of specific genres, namely comics and science fiction. In the opening essay, Martin Barker studies that most fragmented of audiences – the individual reader. He concentrates on the responses of an Australian fan of Judge Dredd who identifies himself as a fascist. In Barker's view, this fan transgresses the boundaries of the usual fan response. He appropriates Dredd as a hero, disregarding the dominant assumption that the comic satirises Dredd's police state, in order to explore imaginatively his significance to his own world view. Barker insists that the relation between comic and fan is more complex than that suggested by the 'media effects' tradition. The fascist fan is neither simply 'influenced' by the comic, nor a 'bad reader' of it; he uses Dredd to negotiate a political understanding.

Imelda Whelehan and Esther Sonnet consider how the appeal of the Tank Girl graphic narratives, created by men, transcends the expected comic readership of post-adolescent, heterosexual 'lads'. Tank Girl's butch image has been appropriated by a young lesbian readership as both an object of fantasy and an icon of powerful womanhood. The plurivocality of the comic text, however, is closed off in its translation into the Hollywood film *Tank Girl* (1995), with its unilinear plot and redefinition of her femininity. Tank Girl's intertextual identity is compounded by advertisers' appropriation of her image as 'post-feminist' woman, capitalising on her transgressive stance to sell once counter-cultural, now mainstream products like jeans. Personal reading is nothing if not political.

Helen Merrick reviews critical work on feminist science fiction and its readership and suggests further directions for research. Arguing that feminist critics have tended to limit themselves to literary/textual approaches to women and SF, she calls for a more broadly-based cultural studies model which takes account of readers' extratextual involvement in the genre and their active role in producing SF. This interactive relationship between fans and culture is, for Merrick as for other contributors, a paradigm of active consumption rather than the exceptional behaviour of fringe obsessives.

Sympathising with these reconsiderations of audiences, Paul Watson explores the limitations of film theory in studying the low-budget sensationalist world of exploitation cinema. He draws on Bourdieu to show how restrictive notions of taste have both shaped film criticism and worked to marginalise exploitation as 'Other' in histories of the cinema. Yet film itself, he argues, has always been about exploiting audiences; the distinction between exploitation and the mainstream is artificial, socially constructed and theoretically disabling. Steve Chibnall and Mikita Brottman, by contrast, explore the aesthetics of individual exploitation films. Chibnall sets *The Flesh and Blood Show* (1972), a splendidly titled British horror film, in the context of the recent enthusiasm for cult and trash films, exploring why such an unexpectedly subtle and thematically rich movie should have attracted neither critical interest nor a substantial cult reputation. Like Merrick, he suggests that distinctions are breaking down between academics and fans, with fans contributing decisively to the revision of the cinematic canon in favour of the popular and transgressive. Brottman considers the psychoanalytic implications of the monster in William Castle's *The Tingler* (1959), which feeds upon fear and can only be expelled by a scream. Castle seeks to manipulate the audience directly, to the extent of installing electric buzzers under cinema seats to jolt unwary spectators during frightening scenes. However, as Brottman shows, audience responses to the film remain varied and unpredictable, evading the director's control.

Continuing the emphasis on horror and popular response, Ian Conrich examines the curiously friendly relationship between audiences and Freddy Krueger, the murderous antihero of the *Nightmare on Elm Street* films. He asks why toys and other merchandising spin-offs from films about a child killer – films apparently designed for a late teenage to adult audience – should have proved so popular among young children. He demonstrates that Freddy achieved a mythic status beyond the films, as a kind of bizarre father figure, and that the films encourage the viewers' (and future toy-buyers') involvement through seductive confusions of illusion and reality.

Translations between genres and media and the consequent transformation of their meanings and potential audiences are the focus for Steve Cramer in studying the novel and film of *The Shining* (novel, 1977; film, 1980). Stanley Kubrick's version of Stephen King's story shifts not only the emphasis between the characters and genre, but the political agenda as well. Cramer notes that whereas the novel plays on an intertextuality with other Gothic fiction, the film's intertextuality lies in its cinematic relationship with a particular horror subgenre, the haunted house film. The haunted house film highlights the female as central character, usually the cause of corruption through her sexuality. However, Kubrick alters King's portrayal of the wife and mother by making Shelley Duvall's Wendy Torrance a locus for a positive, if often comic, female strength. According to Cramer, Jack Nicholson's Jack becomes a monster not because he cannot accept King's right-wing views of the family and the work ethic, but because he insanely *appropriates* these values rather than Kubrick's liberal view.

While the preceding essays focus on some non-traditional genre in comics and exploitation films, their concern is still for mainstream media – print and visual. The concluding piece in this volume takes a further step into new postmodern popular forms. Roberta Pearson extends traditional academic cultural studies research into the cyberspace of the World Wide Web by looking at how computer-mediated communication affects fan culture for Sherlock Holmes enthusiasts on the Internet. Here she finds an international, intertextual, interdisciplinary fandom whose diverse appropriations of Conan Doyle's hero display a range of interests from traditional historicism to feminism. The 'Hounds of the Internet' share and discuss information on Victorian culture, making use of the new technology of the computer much as their hero relied on his quirkily arranged commonplace books as reference sources, but at the same time, their use of the new technology changes their relations within fandom and with Holmesiana itself.

In this multimedia age, barriers are eroded between film and fiction and between elite and popular culture: director's cuts, never seen at the cinema, are now available on laser disk, including critical commentary with the film.[12] Films like *Braveheart* (1995) spawn CD-ROM interactive adaptations,[13] *Babylon 5* creator, J. Michael Straczynski, corresponds with fans on the Internet but warns them not to discuss potential future plots lest he be sued for using any of their ideas.[14] Audiences' experiences of, and interactions with, texts are rapidly evolving and becoming ever more complex. Such developments in popular culture will demand a reconsideration of current theories of audience response in both literature and media studies and the essays in this collection form a part of such a re-examination of audiences' involvement in (re)creating the meanings of filmic and fictional texts.

Notes

1. This is a cliché, of course, but it may have originated with the *Guardian*'s Suzanne Moore (anecdotal evidence).
2. For example, by Jim McGuigan, *Cultural Populism* (London: Routledge, 1992).
3. See, for example Niall Ferguson, 'Oxford? Sorry prof, I'm into media studies', *Independent*, 1 January 1996, p. 17; Nick Tate, the Government's chief advisor on the school curriculum, quoted in Judith Judd, 'Spelling to "come before TV soaps"', *Independent*, 2 May 1996, p. 4.
4. Helen Wilkinson defends popular culture and Media studies against Tate, 'You can't separate Blur from Schubert', *Independent*, 9 February 1996, p. 12.
5. See David Bordwell, *Making Meaning: Inference and Rhetoric in the Interpretation of Cinema* (Cambridge, MA: Harvard University Press, 1989).
6. Pierre Bourdieu, *Distinction: A Social Critique of the Judgement of Taste* (London: Routledge, 1989).
7. Philip French, 'The cinematic equivalent of a Big Mac', *Observer*, 11 August 1996, Review, p. 1.
8. According to Brian Masters, *The Shrine of Jeffrey Dahmer* (London: Hodder and Stoughton, 1993), p. 98.
9. Barbara Creed, *The Monstrous-Feminine: Film, Feminism, Psychoanalysis* (London: Routledge, 1993), pp. 16–30.
10. It is striking that the popular stereotype of the nerdish 'fan' – 'anal', socially inept and badly dressed – neatly coincides with that of the academic.

11. Stanley Fish, *Is There a Text in This Class? The Authority of Interpretive Communities* (Cambridge, MA: Harvard University Press, 1980).
12. For example, the laser disk of Kevin Costner's *Dances with Wolves* (Pioneer, 1991) offers an extended version of the theatrically-released film; Richard Attenborough's *Chaplin* (Pioneer, 1991) includes backstage interviews on the making of the film and Robert Downey's screen test along with the film.
13. The *Braveheart* CD-ROM (Midisoft, 1995) contains not only an hour of video clips from the film and its production and information about its stars, but also historical background on life in William Wallace's Scotland, music and art from the period and games to be played, thereby mixing education and entertainment, high and low culture via the new technology.
14. Susan Clerc, 'Estrogen brigades and "big tits" threads: media fandom online and off', in Lynn Cherny and Elizabeth Reba Weise (eds), *Wired Women: Gender and New Realities in Cyberspace* (Seattle: Seal Press, 1996), p. 91.

Further Reading

Ang, Ien, *Watching Dallas: Soap Opera and the Melodramatic Imagination* (London: Methuen, 1985).

——, *Living Room Wars: Rethinking Media Audiences for a Postmodern World* (London: Routledge, 1996).

Bacon-Smith, Camille, *Enterprising Women: Television Fandom and the Creation of Popular Myth* (Philadelphia: University of Pennsylvania Press, 1992).

Barr, Marleen S., *Feminist Fabulation: Space/Postmodern Fiction* (Iowa City: University of Iowa Press, 1992).

——, *Lost in Space: Probing Feminist Science Fiction and Beyond* (Chapel Hill: North Carolina University Press, 1993).

Baudrillard, Jean, *The Ecstasy of Communication* (New York: Semiotext(e), 1988).

Bennett, Tony and Janet Woollacott, *Bond and Beyond: The Political Career of a Popular Hero* (London: Macmillan, 1987).

Bordwell, David, *Making Meaning: Inference and Rhetoric in the Interpretation of Cinema* (Cambridge, MA: Harvard University Press, 1989).

Bourdieu, Pierre, *Distinction: A Social Critique of the Judgement of Taste* (London: Routledge, 1986).

Buckingham, David (ed.), *Reading Audiences: Young People and the Media* (Manchester: Manchester University Press, 1993).

Cherny, Lynn and Elizabeth Reba Weise (eds), *Wired Women: Gender and New Realities of Cyberspace* (Seattle: Seal Press, 1996).

De Certeau, Michel, *The Practice of Everyday Life* (Berkeley: University of California Press, 1984).

Docherty, David, David Morrison and Michael Tracey, *The Last Picture Show? Britain's Changing Film Audiences* (London: BFI, 1987).

Everman, Welch, *Cult Horror Films* (New York: Citadel Press, 1993).

Featherstone, Mike and Roger Burrows (eds), *Cyberspace, Cyberbodies, Cyberpunk: Cultures of Technological Embodiment* (London: Sage, 1995).

Hartwell, David, *Age of Wonders: Exploring the World of Science Fiction* (New York: Walker Publishing, 1984).

Hollows, Joanne and Mark Jancovich (eds), *Approaches to Popular Film* (Manchester: Manchester University Press, 1995).

Horn, Maurice, *Women in the Comics* (New York: Chelsea House Publishers, 1977).

James, Edward, *Science Fiction in the Twentieth Century* (Oxford: Oxford University Press, 1994).

Jaworzyn, Stefan (ed.), *Shock Express* (London: Titan Books, 1992).

Jenkins, Henry, *Textual Poachers: Television Fans and Participatory Culture* (London: Routledge, 1992).

Jones, Steven G. (ed.), *Cybersociety: Computer-Mediated Communication and Community* (Thousand Oaks: Sage, 1995).

Lewis, Lisa A. (ed.), *The Adoring Audience: Fan Culture and Popular Media* (London: Routledge, 1992).

McCarty, John (ed.), *The Sleaze Merchants: Adventures in Exploitation Film Making* (New York: St Martin's Press, 1995).

Moores, Shaun, *Interpreting Audiences: the Ethnography of Media Consumption* (London: Sage, 1993).

Morley, David, *Television, Audiences and Cultural Studies* (London: Routledge, 1992).

Peary, Danny, *Cult Movies* (New York: Delta Books, 1981).

Penley, Constance, 'Feminism, psychoanalysis and the study of popular culture' in Lawrence Grossberg et al. (eds), *Cultural Studies* (London: Routledge, 1992), pp. 479–500.

Radway, Janice, *Reading the Romance: Women, Patriarchy and Popular Culture* (London: Verso, 1987).

Reynolds, Richard, *Superheroes* (London: Batsford, 1992).

Rheingold, Harold, *The Virtual Community: Homesteading on the Electronic Frontier* (Reading, MA: Addison-Wesley, 1993).

Roof, Judith and Robyn Wiegman (eds), *Who Can Speak? Authority and Critical Identity* (Urbana: University of Illinois Press, 1995).

Sabin, Roger, *Adult Comics: An Introduction* (London: Routledge, 1993).

Schoell, William, *Stay Out of the Shower: The Shocker Film Phenomenon* (London: Robinson, 1988).

Spender, Dale, *Nattering on the Net* (Melbourne: Spinifex, 1995).

Telotte, J.P. (ed.), *The Cult Film Experience* (Austin: University of Texas Press, 1991).

Tulloch, John and Henry Jenkins, *Science Fiction Audiences: Watching Doctor Who and Star Trek* (London and New York: Routledge, 1995).

Warner Jr, Harry, *All Our Yesterdays: An Informal History of SF Fandom in the Forties* (Chicago: Advent, 1969).

Waters, John, *Shock Value: A Tasteful Book About Bad Taste* (New York: Dell, 1981).

1

Taking the Extreme Case: Understanding a Fascist Fan of Judge Dredd

Martin Barker

A sad fact about the recent blossoming of audience research has been how little it has penetrated public understandings of the media. Instead, as recurrent scares have shown, debates still focus around naive questions about 'effects' which most researchers long since thought they had put out with the rubbish. There are many reasons for this failure – not least our own sheer inability, even unwillingness, to get our researches and arguments widely noticed. But I believe that another significant reason is that it must appear that the two sides are talking about different kinds of audience. First, for a complex of reasons, most recent audience research has centred on women's genres.[1] Most of this has concerned itself with the kinds of media materials that are greeted with what we might call 'friendly contempt'. The classic cases are soap operas, romances and genre science fiction. In just a few cases, such studies have begun to deal with more risky materials and have revealed complex group structures, and elaborate practices and motives for involvement.[2]

All these have been very important, without question. But there are gaps. There has been much less interest in uses of media by men – unless it be men's use of pornography. And of course that topic has been the site of deep and angry splits among feminists.[3] Yet it is primarily media involving men that current panics address. Also, all the above studies are about recuperating media uses as 'good things': what had been judged negative, is in fact positive. Soaps, romances, and so on, may look trivial and thin, but in fact they constitute rich materials to their devoted audiences, and meet real needs.

Public concerns about audiences focus around the twin words 'vulnerable' and 'violent'. The vulnerable are those who

14

do not have the social, moral or mental resources to ward off dangerous influences. The violent are those who, for whatever reason, have gone looking for materials to confirm and enhance their viciousness. These are the ones who *might* use *Romper Stomper* (1992) or *Child's Play 3* (1992) or *Natural Born Killers* (1994). These, current research has hardly addressed.

I believe that we have played too safe. Of course, stepping out into these worlds is not comfortable, for many reasons. Recent feminist methodological debates underline this. A central tenet seems to be that the researcher must acknowledge the social relations s/he has with her/his objects of study. That is surely right. But that has been taken to mean that we are in the business of empowering audiences, that we ought even to like them. What do you do if, among the people you are studying, there is someone whom you heartily, and with good reason, dislike?

Putting it at its strongest, what to do if a person you are studying declares himself to be a fascist? Around 1992 I was conducting some research into the readers of the British comic *2000AD*, and its central character Judge Dredd. The scenario of Dredd is relevant: a semi-SF story, it is set in a futuristic, post-nuclear New York called Megacity One. The 400 million population are almost all unemployed, and every social evil and bizarreness (from crime to body-sculpting, to game shows) of our own time has been multiplied to the nth degree. Dredd combines the roles of law-maker, policeman, jury, jailer and (frequently) executioner. The stories, as John Newsinger has shown, shift restlessly from the bleakly political, through the epic and Gothic, to the surreal and humorous.[4] Textually, then, Dredd himself can be shown to be a sardonic antihero within stories which have a satirical twist.

In the course of a pilot exercise, I received four tapes. One was from an Australian whom I will call 'David Smith'. The tape was lucid, clear and responsive. Smith spoke willingly and at considerable length about himself, his life and his reading habits. Half way into the tape, he declared himself a fascist, and laughed at the revelation; and followed this at various points with comments on his love of Nazi books. He then credits Judge Dredd as a major source of inspiration. I hope the challenge is clear: how can one credit Smith's admission of the power of this text without dissolving him into it? Is the text rescuable as 'really satirical' even if Smith declines this reading? Why *shouldn't* this return me to a causal model I otherwise dismiss?

Everything that follows is tentative. I only have a 90-minute tape of his views, and I acknowledge the risks in forming wide judgements on that basis. It could turn out that, for instance, were I to interview him in depth, the term 'fascist' would prove to be an ironic self-ascription, or a gesture of refusal, or something else completely. Frankly, I don't want to interview him further to find out.

As a researcher I acknowledge a number of responsibilities to anybody whom I interview. Among these, I recognise the priest-like rule of confidentiality. I acknowledge the need to deal fully and systematically with any materials I am studying, and also to take account of all the ways in which the research process itself may have altered or constructed the materials I am studying. I acknowledge that as a researcher I stand in a number of privileged relations to any respondent. And I acknowledge that to publish my findings is to put to use – in ways I can control only partially, and my respondents not at all – knowledge about someone else's life and ideas.

What I will not do, is enter into anything approaching a contract with David Smith. A wider politics overrides any obligations I have as a researcher. Yet there are important things to be learnt from just one tape like this, even if they can only question the existing agenda. I wish to maintain my opposition to the 'moral panics' agenda about the media, even at the point of the 'vulnerable' and the 'violent'.[5] It is *still* a gross misunderstanding of how people use the media, and I wish to use David Smith's tape as my argument for this conclusion.

David Smith is a postman in a large Australian city. Twenty-six years old at the time (1992) of communicating with me, he is married to a 22-year-old woman, 'Mary'. They bought their house four years ago, one originally built for railway workers. Smith describes the area where they live: 'The area where I live at the moment is sort of ... um [long pause] sort of I suppose lower, it's lower, I suppose you'd call it lower class, working class basically.'

I use this first direct quotation to indicate a problem in analysing a tape like this. What does one make of hesitations, and uncertainties of expression? My schedule of questions had asked what sort of area they lived in, and how he felt about it. Smith's answer hints at an uncertainty or unease about how to depict his area. He is forthright about the house itself, and about the work which he is doing to extend it. He only hesitates over naming the area it is in. It may well be that this and other hesitations on the tape are marks of his awareness of my probable higher status. To call himself 'lower class' might be to demean himself in front of me. He has never met me, therefore his image of me must be largely fictive, derived mainly from how I wrote to him and from the general social status attached to 'academic research'. I want to suggest that his hesitations indicate an unwillingness to 'name' himself as working class, something that emerges also from his relations with his parents. Yet in the end he will, because of another commitment. This is his desire to deal with things 'sociologically'.

Smith, the oldest of five children, does not get on with his parents. 'Simple answer to your question, I had no intention of getting on well with my parents.' His father is a street sweeper and his mother organises bread deliveries to supermarkets. Leaving home young, he lived with Mary before they married. They have no children yet. The key thing in his life, by his own account, is his reading. Smith reads all the time: 'In fact most people would think that reading is what I do for a living, and my job sorts of helps pay for my reading – it comes pretty close to it sometimes.' His reading is mainly novels – war novels, crime and spy novels (this last only recently). He particularly likes books that he thinks of as 'Nazi books' – though he never identifies exactly what he means by these.

Several times on the tape, Smith insists on his right to read these. Answering a question on whether he thinks fans of other kinds of comics or films are the same as himself, he says,

No I don't believe they are. Probably there are times when I feel maybe they're a bit narrow-minded if that's all they want to read or something but I think that the personal choice factor, the same as I wouldn't like people telling me that I shouldn't read Nazi books, that'd be the same as saying, you know, well, you can't read Jewish books if you're a German or something.

If we take this seriously, not only has he criticised 'fans' for their narrow reading, but also his 'Nazi books' constitute the *opposite* of narrowness. But at the same time that becomes the basis of a defence of their right to read what they choose (the 'personal choice factor'); and this in its turn is illustrated by the right to read Jewish books if you are a German. If there is a criterion behind these shifts in his argument, it is one of rejecting censorious authority – even that of his own side.

It is important to Smith that his tastes are wide. The only reading he positively doesn't like are romances and westerns. Outside those, he reads almost anything. The same with music:

> For instance I like classical music, I also like heavy metal, and I like punk. Why do I like these things? Probably, well, punk naturally enough because it's the one I started off with anyway, probably because of the tongue-in-cheek humour that is hidden in the lyrics, everything being, you know, anti-authoritarian all the time. Heavy metal I like primarily for the musical talent behind it, classical naturally enough it stands alone, on its own, and there's nothing that can beat, compare with classical music of any sort.

And of course Smith loves *2000AD*. Or rather, he loves Judge Dredd. I do not mean by this that he just chooses that story among the several the comic regularly carries. In fact, at various points he does name other *2000AD* stories he likes. No, what is revealing is the way he slides repeatedly in his talk to naming the comic by this one character/scenario. *2000AD* is Judge Dredd, and Judge Dredd is *2000AD*. ('You know, Judge Dredd to me is *the* comic on its own without anything else, right?') In fact, if we can believe his own statements, Dredd surpasses all other reading he does, in remarkable ways. His story of how he came to read the comic is unexceptional:

> Well, basically it was a case of from the age of eight I've been delivering newspapers until I was sixteen or seventeen when

I left school and ... let's see now, *2000AD*, er, Judge Dredd has been going since 1977 ... and probably around 1979, I think I'm correct, around about issue 70 I started regularly buying the comic and, erm, I can't for the life realise why except for the simple fact that it happened to be on the bookshelf at the time at the newsagents that I worked at. And so every Saturday night was pay night and I specifically remember this part of it in particular, and that was the fact that every Saturday night was pay night, and so I'd go, I'd get back from doing my paper round and I'd get paid and I'd go straight over and buy this comic. So I put in a regular order for it and you know I'd go home and I'd sit on the lounge room floor and read it while my parents were watching TV, and we had fish and chips and stuff as the general course of a meal on a Saturday night.

The ordinariness of this is interesting, along with its faintly routine feel – it was a ritual, and part of a wider Saturday night ritual, when the pressures are off and even the food takes on a 'holiday' aspect.

Smith carried on reading Dredd for ten years, from 1978 to 1988. His reading lapsed as his relationship with Mary developed. Then, pressured by lack of space, he asked a good friend, 'Michael', if he would like to buy his set, and perhaps to sell on. (Smith's relationship with his comics was different – he regretted the development of the 'collector' mode among comics' readers. Of Michael he says: 'My only regret is simply the fact that he's more into it from the point of view of keeping each issue purely for the sake of it's worth some money later on. Unfortunately this is one of those factors of the American market.' Real fans don't think of it like that, and in fact suffer because it becomes harder to get the issues they *need*.) Michael bought them all; subsequently the two of them drifted apart.

Friendship blossomed again when the wedding was being planned. Soon they were meeting up fortnightly:

Strangely enough the question came up from me simply from the fact that I'd started to miss Judge Dredd, I'd actually found that I was hooked by it, and I turned around and I'd said, you know, one of the first things I'd said to Michael outside of 'How's the family?' was 'What exactly's going on with Judge Dredd now?' ... And so in, like I said, one thing led to another, I found that I was hooked and wanted to get back into it so Michael started getting me back, started giving me old back issues.

Now Smith buys everything with Dredd in: *2000AD*, *Judge Dredd: The Megazine*, the specials, the US editions, any Titan reprints and so on. Once again he sets ritual time aside for reading them. When he and Mary finally married some six months before he sent me his tape, Michael's wedding present was the complete set he had traded earlier (Mary was not impressed at this one-sided gift!) Smith now knows them encyclopedically. Without ever writing any of it down, he recalls them well enough to be able to recall, for instance, which particular issue contains the panels from which the images of Dredd T-shirts are taken.

What does Dredd mean to Smith? With no doubt a touch of self-mockery, Smith variously calls himself a fan, hooked, obsessed, an addict, a Dreddoholic. 'Judge Dredd to me is like, you know, it's just something, so much, well, let's see, without being blasphemous I suppose it's almost something religious for me.' Here is my dilemma. Smith is a self-named fascist. He tells me what this means for him:

> Strangely enough my father's been proved right in the fact that I actually am a fascist [slight laugh, pause] in my political outlook considering that I can see where Judge Dredd could actually work in some societies or some parts of society. And Michael is the same and so we just talk. We are both fascists in that sense in that we do have a belief in a party-political situation that does rule the country completely, for example, the same as the Justice Department [the machinery of power under which Dredd operates] is in charge of their sort of area.

Being a fascist is for him modelled on something he perceives in Judge Dredd's future-world.

How might we respond? Considering the present condition of audience research, the options seem to be limited to two.

First, we can agree that Smith has indeed used these materials as a ground for his fascism (thus confirming his self-description). In that case, *2000AD* itself comes into question. Either we must conclude that there *is* a fascistic potential in its storylines, and thus move towards the position of the moral panickers; or we might conclude that he has found what he sought, in materials otherwise resistant to such readings – he is the classic case, then, of the sick mind finding sickness in whatever it looks at.

Or, second, we may 'recuperate' him. He calls himself a fascist, but we decide that this marks a discontented response which merely uses Dredd as a token of his resistance. In that sense, he would have something in common with the way the punks have sometimes been spoken of (in, for instance, their borrowing of the swastika symbol). But to argue this, we have to ascribe feelings, needs and aspirations to him to which he himself does not (at least in this tape) admit.

I am not content with these options. First, there is an assumption that reading practices operate between two poles: either 'readers' receive the text's preferred message – in which case, in a sense, they are 'decoded' by the text, and become, subjectively, as the message is – or they are the active generators of meanings out of polysemic texts, making (decoding) meanings according to the requirements and logics of their own social situation. Middle grounds are, of course, possible, but they depend still on the viability of these two poles.

Second, 'reading' is delineated as a complex but nonetheless indivisible process: the act of reading is the act of making meanings. John Corner has sought to question this in a rare investigation of a much-assumed concept. Corner challenges the tendency to conflate several distinct levels of the concept of 'meaning'. The first is the literal recognition of what is said or shown (words, objects, actions, events). The second is the 'connotative' level, grasping that any of these is operating metaphorically or symbolically, and what those connotative additions might be. The third level is wider: 'What does it all mean, and mean to me?', the finding of coherent patterns in which we can anchor ourselves ('The committed attribution of significance, socio-cultural relevance and value').[6] Corner's central point is that these are distinct, may operate differently and indeed conflict with each other in real audiences. It is only their conflation that allows analysts to talk of audiences 'creating their own readings'.

This is well put. But along the way, Corner makes another, more troublesome claim. Turning away from this collapsed notion of 'reading' and 'meaning', he says, requires us to take account of audiences' generic skills, their awareness of what sorts of things they are reading or watching. Pre-eminent among those, he suggests, is the distinction between the factual and the fictional: 'In the former, the viewer is often drawn quite directly into a "response" which involves relations of belief and disbelief, agreement and disagreement. The kinds of text-processing which viewers perform in the two cases are likely to be quite distinctive.'[7] Or as he also puts it:

> the characteristic properties of text–viewer relations in most non-fiction television are primarily to do with kinds of *knowledge*, usually regulated and framed by direct address speech. ... The characteristic properties of text–viewer relations in fictional television are primarily to do with *imaginative pleasure*, particularly the pleasures of dramatic circumstance and of character. [8]

I want to argue that, if true at all, this is only true for 'readers' who have very little *investment* in the media they are using.[9] For those for whom their relationship with chosen materials matters, more complex relations and operations come into play. Put at its simplest, they want to use their stories to purposive ends. With such uses, simplistic separations of the factual and the fictional are unsustainable. This is absolutely not to be read as a contention that people like David Smith 'can't tell the difference between fact and fantasy'. That is precisely wrong. Instead, I draw in particular on Hodge and Tripp's study of how children use and learn from cartoons. They show that young children use cartoons as a way of exploring and elaborating their modalities of fact and fiction.[10]

This, I would argue, has special resonance for studying audiences of works such as *2000AD*, where the imagining of possible futures is at stake. Contra Corner, I want to argue that inasmuch as people do separate 'fact' and 'fiction', this may be a problem, because it means that they do not have available imaginative scenarios of how the world might be different. I believe that a thorough development of the implications of these ideas will require a challenge to many aspects of the prevalent languages within cultural studies' talk about audiences: from the primarily psychoanalytic ways of discussing 'fantasy'; via the celebrations of women readers whose main response to their texts is only to produce more; to the very language of 'texts' and indeed 'metatexts'. I am well aware that these large claims leap way beyond anything I can fully articulate in this chapter, let alone illustrate or test. But they nonetheless provide the general rubric within which I have found myself able to look at David Smith as an 'extreme reader'.

Begin again with David Smith's rejection of romance: 'The reason I don't like romance is simply because it's just pretentious. People, people aren't really the way that they're portrayed in those sort of shows. There's not enough realism, enough reality involved in them.' Smith does not say much more than this, but it is evident that 'realism' and 'reality' are not literal terms.[11] In fact, his own account of Dredd would seem to fall under the same criticism, if we took the term 'realism' literally. Not only is *2000AD* science fiction, but Smith himself says of it that what he likes is its *impossibility*.

Smith is insistent that he is not a 'typical fan'. He is clear what that means for him. A typical fan is into the comic for its *comicness*: the artwork, its telling of stories. That is not his interest in it. Several times, at different points of the tape, Smith tells me that he is interested in the comic for its 'sociological' dimensions. Here is one:

> Like I've already said, I talk about Judge Dredd with Michael on a sociological ... basis really. For instance, one question Michael once said to me once he realised that Judge Dredd was like my sort of like a hero in this world that hasn't got any, anyway it was simply basically a case that he said to me one day we were watching *Friday the 13th Part 8*, 'Jason Takes Manhattan', and Michael turned around and said to me: 'David, what would Judge Dredd do against this guy Jason?' And I just turned round to him and said to him, well,

he'd probably fire a couple of shots at him, provided the guy was still walking, depending on how good the script was this person had given him, of course, and I think, well he'd probably just get onto his bike radio and: 'Give me a H-wagon down here to nuke this guy', end of sequence. So technically we do talk things in that sense, like you know, hypotheticals and so forth, as well as talking on a sociological basis.

This comes immediately before the passage in which Smith tells me that he is a fascist. There is for him a direct link between a discourse about the 'sociology' of the comic, and his self-designation as a fascist.

This isn't the only time he talks of his uses of Dredd as scenario. Just a little earlier, he had answered a question about how non-comic-reading friends respond to his love of it:

I do find he's on my mind quite a bit ... No, well the only reason they know about it is 'cos times at work a particular issue of Judge Dredd will have caught my fancy and it'll be something like, say it's the euthanasia factor or something, and suddenly someone at work will be talking about euthanasia and I'll sit there and suddenly I'll think about Judge Dredd and I'll give a little chuckle and it's quite interesting, they'll ask me, 'What are you laughing about, David?' And I'll turn around and say, 'There's this character in this comic that I read. His name's Judge Dredd.' And I'll give them the storyline based on this euthanasia factor for example, yeah? And they tend to sit there and say 'Oh yeah, alright.'

He is of course well aware of the distinction between 'story' and 'reality', but that is not the point. For the sociological possibilities of the story are that they can set up measures and tests for the explication and rightness of the world as it is. These constitute for him the 'deeper' levels of the comic. He voices his frustration that he can never get the publishers to take seriously their responsibilities in this area. He wants to see more stories exploring these kinds of themes. And he wants the publishers to set up a Judge Dredd Appreciation Society, so that:

we could discuss these ideas, pass them back and forth to each other and stuff like that. I feel that OK, the comics are two-dimensional things but they have introduced, recently *2000AD* have introduced, during the last few years anyway have introduced some psychological and sociological questions that I feel do need to be answered in a sense, for those of us like myself who really need to know more on this society that supposedly he's holding the law in.

The need to know more about this society, the need to understand its dynamics, the need to go deeper, and not just read the stories: these are the constructing criteria for his accounting with Judge Dredd. In a revealing passage he addresses me and defends himself against what he suspects might be my criticism:

> I often find when I read the letter section of *2000AD* that often people are sending their crazy you know stories that to me are boring and just so, so childish. OK people say and yeah, you're probably sitting there and thinking to yourself, Martin, that OK you know, this guy's calling certain readers childish, what about himself? He's been reading them fifteen years, has he nothing else to do in life? I'll admit I am feeling childish at times myself, but I think it might be simply a factor that maybe my imagination, erm, maybe my imagination input doesn't sort of suit the sort of, the sort of information that *2000AD* is giving. Whereas Judge Dredd is something that, is a character that I've grown with and sort of expanded along with. I sort of understand, a sort of feel for the way he's portrayed in the Judge Dredd story in particular. I often don't find that I like some of the fans who are just into the comic itself and not, like, Judge Dredd and the deeper things in Judge Dredd for itself too.

This is discursively quite complicated. When thinking of other readers and the normal reading of the comic, it is called *2000AD*. But his own relationship is via the character of Judge Dredd. 'Childishness' is just the making up of stories. That is not what he does. The distinction he wants to make is between just making up stories, and using your 'imagination' with the 'deeper things' that the comic gives.

So Smith's relationship *is* very much with and via the character. But it is unvaryingly a relationship which begins from and assumes Dredd's fictionality. It comes from two things. First, Dredd rings true in Smith's world – and of course Dredd's world is textually full of references to our own and is in many respects on a continuum with ours. So Smith can complain that the publishers duck out of dealing with some really important contemporary issues, such as sexual violence. It is so significant in our world, therefore it must be dealt with in Dredd's.

But Dredd is more than just a character. He is a measure of something more. I had asked how often in any week he might think about his comics: 'I would have to say that thinking about my typical week I spend a good deal of my time thinking about my comics 'cos I think of different scenarios for Judge Dredd. Judge Dredd is a sort of, he's a universal character. He's a typical example of a cop that can be used in just about any situation.' Being a universal character means a good deal. It is not simply that he takes on ethical dimensions, it means that he has to live up to certain metatextual requirements. Here is how he explores this on the tape:

OK, the reason I like so much, well, Judge Dredd is *the* character, like I said, in *2000AD* as far as I am concerned. Erm. The thing I like about it so much is that he is so incorruptible, and even when he is corrupt, there is some sort of loophole in their legal system, you know, which makes him still the good guy. No matter what, he's still the good guy. And I mean even with these factors like, intimidation is alright, but you can't torture a person for, for their um questions, he can lie, cheat and everything but he cannot beat them up. I think that sort of factor in there, it's, I think it's because the world, the world around us is not black and white anyway, Judge Dredd portrays it as black and white, but even if there's a grey area he suddenly makes it black or white to suit himself. The Justice Department itself is this basic godhead, it's a massive big godhead. Erm. The storylines are always great, I mean, you, it takes the simplest story, you know the writers take the simplest story, like you know, a guy drops litter on the street, he's a classic example, a guy drops litter on the street, Judge Dredd sees him and says, 'Hey you.' The perpetrator runs, in panic, which is a totally wise thing to do considering the sort of world he lives in anyway – runs in panic, knocks over four or five people or whatever, and eventually falls off a balcony while Judge Dredd's still chasing him, falls off a balcony, drops on the ground, has all the broken bones and everything else and has to go through all the hassle of medical expenses and so forth. Judge Dredd just wanted him for one little six months in jail for littering, sort of thing. It's so ironic, that sort of factor behind it.

Notice the return of the religious references, yet so ordinarily married with his awareness of the importance of the writers. An appreciation of story is always more than an appreciation of it as story – it is the enunciation of a world of rules, and of moral power:

From my point of view, I think he'd probably make one of the best chief judges that they would ever have in Megacity One. And yet it's simply a case that he knows that on the streets he's placed, and that's where he feels comfortable. He knows that, like it's sort of like, you know, the cliché factor of, you know, the tough cops they've got on TV, Dirty Harry and the like, and then you know, on the street with all the action where they do their work, they're not the politicians of the day, sort of thing, and yet really they are the political power of the day.

The key is that Dredd must be pure, even if the price of that is some contradiction with the actual rules of the story-world. In *Smith's* interpretative world, no contradiction occurs:

I find that with the likes of Judge Dredd, it's simply a case that he's so, he's so incorruptible. ... [N]ot long ago just before he took his, before he resigned and took his Long Walk, he erm, he let out the members of the Democratic Front. You know, because by a child's questioning of what was so

wrong with the democratic system seemed to have put some
sort of twinge in him. And he even came back afterwards,
after he'd been out on the Long Walk and all, came back
and said to the senior judges after Necropolis when they
started cleaning things up a bit, walked in and said well, why
don't we give them, the people, the right to vote? I mean,
I'm surprised that *2000AD* hasn't expanded on that story,
I feel that there's a lot more there that they could really
expand the character, I'm afraid they're sort of hitting below
the mark when they're not prepared to do that. I mean, to
me I feel personally that now when there is this factor that
they could put in, like, we're all sitting there waiting to see
just how is Dredd going to change. He's becoming more
human. Strangely enough, he's become more human as
the stories are going along.

Smith stands outside the comic and makes sure, while he
enjoys it, that it meets his criteria. The fact that Dredd, the
embodiment of law, was actually worried about the purity of
the law only serves to confirm his judgement. He smells the
story's potential to present what he feels he needs: the
embodiment of a solution to things that are wrong around him,
a model of power and probity. And his own capacity to see
these things confirms what he thought, that he has the
necessary 'deep imagination' to see to the bottom of things.
And that means that he can comment with largesse on the
developments of which he approves, much in the mode of a
literary critic.

I like David Smith no more, having explored his tape, than
I did before. But there is much to be learnt from his account
of himself. He *is* influenced by Judge Dredd, there is no reason
to deny him this. And that influence does reinforce a tendency,
which we may as well call 'fascist', towards believing in some
total police-state. But what shows in his discourse is a search
for an ethical ideal which has found some cultural materials
which, precisely because of their real textual characteristics,
he can use as a resource. That is how real thinking goes. And
that brings me full circle to my opening query about his
hesitations over 'class'. My suspicion is that that hesitation
underlines the fact that Smith is poised between two different
ideological accounts of the world: an authoritarian/fascist

approach; and a socialist rejoinder. Given his life circumstances, a settled choice might never be made – I can't know. But if ever I were to meet my respondent, my goal would be to argue with *him* about visions of a future world, not to cleanse him of some wayward media influence. At such a point, analysis stops; and the real relations of committed researchers to the world they inhabit have to kick in.

Notes

1. The range of such work is considerable, though not as large as might seem at first sight. There have been a number of recent summaries; see for instance, Shaun Moores, *Interpreting Audiences: The Ethnography of Media Consumption* (London: Sage, 1993) and David Morley, *Television, Audiences and Cultural Studies* (London: Routledge, 1992).
2. See some of the essays collected in Lisa A. Lewis (ed.), *The Adoring Audience: Fan Culture and Popular Media* (London: Routledge, 1992); Constance Penley, 'Feminism, psychoanalysis and the study of popular culture', in Lawrence Grossberg et al. (eds), *Cultural Studies* (London: Routledge, 1992), pp. 479–500; and Camille Bacon-Smith, *Enterprising Women: Television Fandom and the Creation of Popular Myth* (Philadelphia: University of Pennsylvania Press, 1992).
3. See the arguments brought together in Alison Assiter and Avedon Carol (eds), *Bad Girls and Dirty Pictures: The Challenge to Reclaim Feminism* (London: Pluto Press, 1993) and Pamela Church Gibson and Roma Gibson (eds), *Dirty Looks: Women, Pornography and Power* (London: BFI Books, 1993).
4. John Newsinger, 'The Dredd phenomenon', *Foundation* 52 (1988).
5. I should be clear that I do not have any reason to suppose that David Smith is an active fascist, who has ever used violence as part of his politics. He says of himself at one point:

> Like I say to myself, I should be a philosopher. I'm from the Nietzsche school of philosophy as it were, in that

> I don't give a stuff basically [laughs]. But I do have a friend that comes round on a fairly regular basis and we talk on several subjects, Nazism, philosophy, etc. and *Dr Who* is another one we get into, and Judge Dredd sort of slips in there quite regularly when I want to talk about him and it's just one of those things.

6. John Corner, 'Meaning, genre and context: the problematics of "public knowledge" in the new audience studies', in James Curran and Michael Gurevitch (eds), *Mass Media and Society* (London: Edward Arnold, 1991), pp. 267–84. This quotation, p. 275. See also Martin Barker, 'Seeing how you can see: on being a fan of *2000AD*', in David Buckingham (ed.), *Reading Audiences: Young People and the Media* (Manchester: Manchester University Press, 1993), pp. 129–83.
7. Corner, 'Meaning, genre and context', p. 272.
8. Ibid., p. 276.
9. The concept of 'investment' cannot be elaborated here to anything like the extent it needs. It has emerged as a key explanatory term in the research currently I am (mid-1996) completing for the ESRC on the audiences for the film version of *Judge Dredd*.
10. Robert Hodge and David Tripp, *Children and Television: A Semiotic Approach* (Cambridge: Polity Press, 1986).
11. For one of the best expositions of this, see Ien Ang, *Watching Dallas: Soap Opera and the Melodramatic Imagination* (London: Methuen, 1985).

2

Regendered Reading: Tank Girl and Postmodernist Intertextuality

Imelda Whelehan and Esther Sonnet

The launch of 'Tank Girl' via *Deadline* magazine in 1988 coincided with a boom period for adult comics which promised a new era for a genre which, in common with other 'debased' areas of popular culture, had only recently been taken seriously and treated to the same kind of critical scrutiny as other popular forms. Even though, as Roger Sabin points out,[1] the view that the adult comic 'arrived' on the scene in the 1980s is a myth, it is true that this period saw significant developments within the genre which reflected the emergence of a new readership both more sophisticated and more heterogeneous than had traditionally been identified.[2] This suggests that the success of 'Tank Girl' lay in some part with meeting an increased demand for new, more challenging examples *within* the adult comics genre, but also signals wider processes in the dissemination of 'underground' forms within the mainstream media scene. One of the major influences on the wider readership for 'Tank Girl' was the increased accessibility of the comic itself as mainstream publishers Penguin produced a collected edition of stories in book form. Hollywood also picked up on the new audiences for comic book characters and narratives and, most spectacularly, began a series of *Batman* adaptations in 1989. With the film version released in 1995, Tank Girl's progress from magazine strip to published book-length volume to Hollywood movie seems in this context a natural one, but what is particularly interesting about the Tank Girl image, however, was its availability for readers across a variety of locations: comic strip, film, the Internet and more broadly within style culture.

31

While testament to the rather surprising success within the mainstream of a super antiheroine created by two British men, Jamie Hewlett and Alan Martin, the intertextual quality of Tank Girl (as cultural image) sets up some difficult questions around the relations between audiences and the reception of popular cultural forms. It is not our aim to attempt primary research of these audiences; instead we intend to look at the implied readers and viewers of Tank Girl in different media, by means of analysing the modes of address utilised and implied, and the fate of the meanings generated and accumulated by the Tank Girl image in its dispersal over several cultural sites. In this sense, the multiple 'texts' of Tank Girl are symptomatic of a popular cultural scene dominated by the aesthetics of postmodernist intertextuality and bricolage. However, our analysis is underpinned by a concern for the fate of gender and sexual difference within contemporary intertextual practices, and for questions of audience within those popular textual forms which inhabit a 'postmodernist' and 'post-feminist' cultural environment. As Barbara Klinger observes:

The intense intertextual environment of mass culture ... is not simply a context full of free-floating signifiers that can be operated by members of society as they will; mass culture also embodies a series of ideological procedures accompanying textual production that bear significantly on reception.[3]

To begin: what model of intertextuality best explains the different ways in which gender and sexual differences operate across the varying cultural locations of 'Tank Girl'? Barbara Klinger notes two formulations for grasping the notion of intertextuality. The first is a post-structuralist and predominantly literary one, associated with Umberto Eco and Roland Barthes, which distinguishes between 'open' and 'closed' texts. The 'closed' work is semiotically limited by its overall structure: classical realist works, for example, are held to be 'closed' because they depend on formulaic narratives and strictures of realism, psychological coherence and plot closure. 'Open' texts, by contrast, foreground intertextuality, which functions as a marker of the semiotically heterogeneous. The plurality of meanings and intertextual references of avant-garde 'open' texts takes the reader beyond the confines of the unilinear narrative into the realms of plurivocality and poly-semanticity. But, as many theorists have recognised, behind this seemingly neutral distinction between 'closed' and 'open' texts, a value distinction is being made between, on one side, the transgressive, modernist text and, on the other, the ideologically complicit works of popular genre forms. More pertinently for our discussion, this model of intertextuality correlates the two forms of text/work with two distinct conceptions of the role of the reader. If the modernist 'open' text of *'jouissance'* engages the reader as *active* principle in the generation of textual meaning, the 'closed' work of *'plaisir'* takes the reader along a pre-defined and self-enclosed path of narrative repetition.

But taking the overall cultural proliferation of discourses around/in 'Tank Girl' as exemplary instance, it is clear that the post-structuralist model cannot address how intertextuality might also characterise conventionally 'closed' media forms in ways that challenge any politics of reading based on formal textual strategies as sole determinants of meaning. In short, a second notion of intertextuality within popular cultural forms is required to account for its functioning to radically dissimilar ends than that of 'textual transgression'. Klinger argues for a reception-based model of intertextuality and turns to the work of Tony Bennett and Janet Woollacott who have similarly argued for a 'social theory' of reading. Recognising that intertextuality might better be regarded not simply as formal mechanisms within types of text (quotation, allusion and reference), but more socio-historically as overall semantic context, it is the 'social organisation of the relations between texts within *specific conditions of reading'* (our emphasis)[4] that work to define the postmodern circulation of meaning-making within contemporary media forms. This is important for assessing how heterogeneous audiences are addressed across the cultural sites which form the social context of reception(s) for 'Tank Girl'. With this in mind, it is now timely to consider how the 'original' graphic narrative functions within a semantic field.which, we would argue, works finally to gender its heroine through particular intertextual 'readerships'.

According to Sabin, comics 'have been "borrowed from" by other media to a degree that is extraordinary compared to other areas of the arts',[5] and the Tank Girl image has proved exceptionally malleable to appropriation. Appearing in style magazines from *Vogue* to *Diva*, the character's image defined the visual references of teen-oriented fashion in Miss Selfridge's Summer 1995 collection and was used to sell Wrangler jeans; the film involved high profile – mainly female – figures from the music business such as Bjork, Belly, Courtney Love, Joan Jett and Ice-T (who also plays T-Saint, leader of the mutant kangaroos). Similarly, the comic form, always renowned for its generic reflexivity, translates comfortably to a postmodern intertextuality, infinitely parasitic and perverse in its melange of images, styles and references. Although individual comic episodes retain a vague narrative coherence (but one which may be thematic rather than motivational), and although relationships between Tank Girl and other figures such as the kangaroo Booga are developed across episodes as the character progresses, storylines are discontinuous and the identity of Tank Girl is itself fragmented. Sometimes the 'story' in an episode never seems to get off the ground (in terms of cause, function and effect) as the point becomes a self-referential account of authorial inertia, or dramatisation of the artist's conflict with his own creation. References can become increasingly arcane, and interestingly, Anglocentric (such as references to DJs/presenters Mike Smith, Timmy Mallett and Keith Chegwin).

If the normal readership for such comics is, as Sabin suggests, supposedly post-adolescent men, then at another level the implied receiver of the authorial address framing the comic strip is much older, if references to children's TV classics like *The Banana Splits* are taken as evidence. This is further reinforced by the introduction of fictional identities and narrative roles for both creators, Hewlett and Martin, portrayed as reluctant celebrities preferring to live anonymously in their home town of Worthing. The 'Australian-ness' of Tank Girl remains unexplained and anachronistic,[6] although it seems to spawn a number of references to the Australian soap *Neighbours*,[7] this in itself historically places the inception of 'Tank Girl' at the height of British TV's (and by implication the British popular audience's) love-affair with Australian soaps. The non-linear qualities of narrative and 'knowing' allusions to other cultural discourses of TV, popular music and cinema mark the comic as deconstructive, openly declaring its status as a fictional construct and foregrounding its popular cultural locatedness. And it is through these that the 'Tank Girl' comic conjures up an identifiable 'style' presence by 'borrowing' from a heady mixture of contemporary styling and nostalgia. As Sabin suggests, *Deadline* was one of a group of magazines known as '"style comics", due to their blend of strips and elements from the style magazines – notably modish presentation and music coverage'.[8] The term 'style comic' perhaps also suggests that comic consumption could be a new kind of style statement in itself, a point reinforced by the fact that 'the *Face*, *iD* and the *Cut* all commissioned integral adult comic strips'.[9] From the allocation of specific rock 'soundtracks' to selected strips, to the Doc Marten and bra-wearing heroine (clearly redolent of a late 1980s personification of Madonna), it is the case that the visual and verbal references of 'Tank Girl' located it firmly within contemporary notions of 'style'. More specifically, what the comic presentation enacts is a female style which is rooted in the performance of female power and it is this which, we would argue, opens up the comic 'text' to different constituencies of readers. From the central fact that the protagonist is a female mythic hero, it is crucial to question whether the historically male-defined conditions of readership and creation within the adult comic tradition position her simply as an object of heterosexual male desire, or whether 'Tank Girl' has opened up the traditional post-adolescent male market to proactive female and/or feminist negotiation, and thus also to female readers who may use strategies which transcend conventional modes of 'reading'.

In response to the issue of the construction of Tank Girl as object of heterosexual male desire, it is clear that the lack of any substantial precedents for female characters as main narrative agents within the adult comic tradition in general is closely allied to the fact that within it representations of female characters are predominantly eroticised. While generic differences between the contemporary adult comics and the 'superheroes' formula popular in the 1940s and 1950s are considerable (not least because Tank Girl eschews magical or superhuman powers) it is nonetheless the case that female characters must make their way against a tradition in which their narrative centrality and agency is overdetermined by their sexualised objectification. In this context, it is worth observing Richard Reynolds' point on the appearance and costume of the 'original' superheroine Wonder Woman. He notes that she was developed as a 'frank appeal to male fantasies of sexual domination' as 'disingenuously set forth' by her creator (psychologist Dr William Moulton Marston) in the following terms: 'Give them an alluring woman stronger than themselves to submit to and they'll be proud to be her willing slaves.'[10] Thus while Tank Girl's healthy disrespect for male power might be viewed in terms of a dismantling of masculine norms, the character's creation by men (in common with the male creation of the also popular Halo Jones in *2000AD*) sets up tensions here, reminding us that the style comics of the 1990s remain resolutely male-identified. While resisting the evidently untenable position that the gender of a creative artist in any sense 'guarantees' the political meaning of the work, it is significant that comics produced by women in the 1970s offering stridently feminist revisions, such as *It Ain't Me Babe,* rarely even survive at the subcultural level, let alone the glossy mainstream (though individual artists such as Julie Hollings have appeared in *Deadline*).[11] In this context, 'Tank Girl' clearly does not offer a narrative portrayal of female experience, but rather remains bound up with the masochistic pleasures of male fantasies of powerful female figures.

This reading receives further support if the audience for 'Tank Girl' is extended to include the Internet – a communication network quintessentially defined by its multiplication of potentialities for extratextual 'readership' activities which simultaneously demonstrate a fidelity to and irreverence for Tank Girl's textual origins. Here, 'Tank Girl' homepages on the Internet include a substantial presence on the World Wide Web of one British aficionado, Bob Rosenberg, offering several pages dealing with the 'history' of 'Tank Girl', a display of pictures downloaded from the comics, a gallery of Tank Girl lookalikes, and an account of the production of the film version. In addition the Internet Movie Database lists the cast and gives other information, while also providing access to a number of individual film reviews – all bar one of which seem to have been written by men. In fact all mentions of her 'cult following' are distinctly male-oriented, and Bob Rosenberg on the Net reveals that 'rock stars from Adam Ant and Billy Bragg to The Ramones and New Order loved her and were keen to be involved in the magazine. Actors and comedians like Lenny Henry and Jonathan Ross were in awe of her.'[12] This seems to be borne out by the blurb on the second Penguin collection which offers testimonies from Henry, Ross and Adam Ant. Rosenberg has a clear investment with Tank Girl's 'sassiness', characterising her (as Hewlett and Martin themselves seem to do) as the rebellious and thankless child of her creators, and celebrates the 'original' Tank Girl – despite his own contradictory acknowledgement that the creators, jaded by success, 'subverted the character at every turn'.[13] His allusion to a troubled relationship between creators and creation re-enacts gendered tensions, borne out by Frank Wynne in his masculinisation of the reader/viewer as he suggests that Tank Girl would 'spit in your eye and kick you in the nuts if you said different'.[14]

It may, though, be a little precipitate to characterise the readership of 'Tank Girl' as male solely on the basis of Internet use given that, as writers such as Dale Spender have observed, it is generally a field of communication 'where aggression, intimidation and plain macho-mode prevail'.[15] Indeed, our concern is with the ways in which the audiences for 'Tank Girl' *cannot* be homogeneously construed and, in this respect, her emergence as a style icon is intriguing for the manner in which the character also offers moments of contradiction and resistance to the culturally dominant mode of representation. This seems to signal some textual space for envisioning a female, perhaps feminist, readership. In one episode, Tank Girl discovers that her creators have cut holes in her bra; she chides them for the puerile transparency of their attempts to undress and thus to objectify her. She refuses to remain topless and, in true deconstructive style, the comic strip is resolved by her wearing two strategically placed pieces of paper with 'censored' written upon them thoughout the remainder of the narrative until, interestingly, at the strip's conclusion it is the reader rather than creators who are addressed: 'I guess you tight fisted heterosexuals will have to buy the next issue to see the outcome.'[16] While her creators are declaring their own knowingness about the sexualised consumption of the female body, the reader is left in this final address as presumably male. Returning the sexualising gaze back to its 'origin' with the creators, the character simultaneously addresses her male audience's complicity and subverts the 'naturalness' of the traditional structure of looking within the genre. A complex negotiation of meanings is thus set up by the inescapably gendered conventions at work in reading a male-created female figure within a traditionally male-defined genre.

As Martin Barker has commented, 'Readers learn what to expect, and what is expected of them. This is how they can recognise when their expectations are being disappointed. And perhaps those disappointments can be our best evidence of what those typified expectations were.'[17] In doing so, the Tank Girl figure successfully crystallises ideas on gender, power and appearance in what has been termed the era of 'post-feminist' politics and cultural critique. If Tank Girl's image is positioned within the discourse of so-called 'post-feminism', her resemblance to Madonna – a major embodiment of the contemporary image of the 'powerful female' – is obvious. Just as Madonna's image has been variously seen as 'empowering', as an ironic appropriation of traditional feminine attire for 'feminist' purposes, so Tank Girl's skinhead glamour might be regarded as setting a new 'degendered' and transgressive mould. This would neatly encapsulate contemporary registrations of the 'fact' that 1970s feminism has been superseded and rendered delegitimate by a new power politics of assertive individualism and self-possession of sexual style. It would also go some way towards explaining how the comic strip invites a 'look' from the reading constituency for whom the purpose of appropriating the Tank Girl image is resolutely not heterosexual, but *women-identified*.

Anticipating the imminent release of the film (June 1995 in the UK), the June 1995 edition of the lesbian magazine *Diva* addressed the ways in which the 'Tank Girl' strip had always attracted a lesbian audience who 'fell hard for [her] anarchic philosophising, filthy language, aptitude for violence and, err, nice tits'.[18] But while marking out Tank Girl's sartorial style, tomboyish aggressivity and specifically skinhead 'tufty' haircut as lesbian in origin, lesbian readers seem to accept that the comic world is a 'Boy's Own' one. Interestingly, Tank Girl is therefore constructed not as an object of homoerotic desire but as an image to be identified with, a 'bisexual kangaroo shagger' whose 'polymorphous perversity provided a useful emotional loophole for dykes who might not have been taken with an outwardly heterosexual character'.[19] There seems to be an acknowledgement that the 'proper' use of Tank Girl is as a *heterosexual* object of desire, 'even if some of us wanted Tank Girl to be the lesbian she so closely resembled, we knew in our hearts she wasn't'.[20] One young lesbian is reported as describing Tank Girl as

> the boot stomping, shaven-headed, growling grrrl [sic] and the stories were just camped up fantasy, pure and simple. She didn't need a reason to do what she did – it was all about hedonistic enjoyment and that was really appealing to a young dyke back then. It's ironic that while girls were reading the strips and identifying away, like 'Go, Tank Girl!' I think to the boys it was just a form of soft porn.[21]

This suggests that certain female spectators at least interpret the mode of address of the image as being directed at men for sexual consumption, but who are nonetheless capable of appropriating the space of 'the look' in order to occupy the identificatory space of a fantasy of sexualised female power expressed through aggression. Compare this to another aggressive lesbian character, Hothead Paisan,[22] and her vigilante attitudes to crimes against women, who does not solicit a sexual gaze and is therefore judged by *Diva* to have 'all the bad language, psychosis and wit, plus political analysis, but a low crumpet rating'.[23]

Interestingly, lesbians claim the provenance of the Tank Girl image which set up frictions between the lesbian and male 'anorak' comic fans that were manifested in extratextual readership activities: when many 'rowdy young skinhead dykes' turned up to *Deadline* Tank Girl lookalike contests, their obvious three-dimensional dykiness was found to be distinctly unpalatable to a male audience evidently disturbed by a *lesbian* embodiment of 'their' heterosexual fantasy figure. Such clashes of interpretation indicate the importance of recognising the role of the extratextual in accounting for the readership dynamics centred around 'Tank Girl'. This is most significant if we consider how spectatorship operates within the film version, *Tank Girl*. Emerging at the later stages of the accumulation of adaptations of the image (its display in glossy and style magazines, advertising and even its use in the slogan 'Tank Girl Is Out!' by Trade Unions against Section 28),[24] it is clear that the reading constituencies are likely to react differently to the film adaptation of the script. Having explored the various meanings of 'Tank Girl' that a proportion of the film audience might take with them into the cinema, and what locations of the image they depend upon, it is now timely to consider how/if some form of 'recuperation' takes place in order to place the image in a different commercial environment from its subcultural 'origins'.

The filming of *Tank Girl* (begun in June and finished in October 1994) follows the period when, according to Sabin, 'comics were not hip anymore';[25] but its director, Rachel Talalay had some credentials in the cult movie circles as producer of *Hairspray* (1988, directed by John Waters) and even in her direction of the unremarkable tired-out formulaic sequel, *Freddy's Dead: The Final Nightmare* (1991). While the comic's 'style' presence is recuperated through an impressive cast list of musicians and contemporary soundtracks, the film does not seek to capture the comic's hybrid set of popular cultural references – its Anglocentrism would clearly not translate well in the Hollywood medium. Instead, in an attempt to reproduce the extratextual effects of the comic, *cinematic* references abound. Mainly the allusions are to male-defined film genres, using war film conventions, Nazi-style uniforms and Batman 'superhero' quotations, while weaving a James Bond 'special effects' denouement into a narrative model more typical of SF dystopias. These sit alongside references to Hollywood classics such as *The Wizard of Oz* (1939; at the end the adversary Kesslee is sapped of his own bodily fluids and screams, 'I'm melting'; this sequence is followed by a cartoon image of

Dorothy and Toto), and to the Busby Berkeley musical with the use of the female body in geometric and gratuitous display in an equally gratuitous 'production number' of Cole Porter's 'Let's Do It' in the Liquid Silver brothel, where Tank Girl (named Rebecca in the film) goes to save the young child, Sam, from enforced prostitution. Further, the film's opening, accompanied by an explanatory voiceover, creates a more seamless and progressive narrative which even the machine-gun editing and animated intercuts cannot – and do not try to – disrupt. Thus, unlike other textual adaptations – where adapters may be more sensitive to the expectations of authenticity and accuracy brought to the film by a community of erstwhile readers (for example, Jane Austen devotees) – the *Tank Girl* adaptation largely rests on making the cartoon image into flesh and blood: the physical image of the heroine must be 'authentic', to the point that the lead actress must agree to shave her head – something Emily Lloyd, the original choice, refused to do. Lori Petty, the eventual choice, clearly embraces Jamie Hewlett's idea of the Tank Girl persona, as he comments on Hollywood's making over of 'Tank Girl' that 'Visually they came very close, story-wise not at all.'[26]

However, the 'authentic' disrupted and fragmented narrative which makes visual sense in comic form does not translate readily to mainstream Hollywood where action heroes need a motive for their actions. Unlike the comic which clearly centres on Tank Girl as an unheroic or even accidental antihero, whose exploits are just as likely to end in drunkenness, sex or the accidental dismembering of male adversaries, the cinematic version of the protagonist is situated from the outset with an emotional and even moral justification for her future actions. Both comic and film present her as 'outside' the dominant social/economic system, but in the film she is placed in an alternative environment, not unlike a New Age hippie commune, and the landscape is post-apocalyptic with echoes of *Mad Max* and *The Terminator*. This scenario is the result of an environmental disaster (a comet has come in direct collision with earth and caused a shift in the weather, where water, in the absence of any rain, becomes a scarce and valuable commodity). We are confronted with a predictable clash of adversarial interests, where the global monopoly 'Water and

Power' is headed by a demonic ruthless figure, Kesslee (played by Malcolm McDowell); its only rival is the anonymous group of 'Rippers' led by their 'creator' Dr Johnny Prophet. Tank Girl's (Rebecca's) community is seen to live relatively peacefully in a squatter relationship (they illegally siphon water) although the violence of this world is emphasised by their need to keep watch every night. Tank Girl's heroic motivation in this film comes, in classic Western generic style, from her witnessing the slaughter of her boyfriend, her trusty steed (something resembling a water buffalo) and the abduction of one of the commune's children. The destruction of the homestead and her subsequent capture to work in slave-like conditions, prompts her to seek both liberation and revenge. This indicates a major difference in mode of address between the film and the comic, though the pressure for narrative resolution is only one way in which mainstream cinema works to constrict the capacity for 'open', heterogeneous readings of a female narrative protagonist. More significantly, the specific conditions of the medium alter the terms upon which transgressive potential is made available to a heterogeneous readership.

As addressed previously, Tank Girl's image holds parallel with other contemporary 'post-feminist' icons:[27]

> Madonna is the true feminist. She exposes the Puritanism and suffocating ideology of American feminism, which is stuck in an adolescent whining mode. Madonna has taught young women to be fully female while still exercising control over their lives.[28]

As Camille Paglia here suggests, the 'post-feminist' heroine is regarded as transgressive and challenging for depicting a woman 'in control'. We are encouraged to position gender politics on an account of 'control' that rests solely on the view that a certain female style and set of behaviours can operate as ironic and knowing, which can celebrate pre-feminist feminine identity with a playfulness which is both performative and transgressive. There is, of course, a degree of debate about what would constitute a transgressive image, but presumably it must in some way dismantle gender binarism without reviving its essential dynamics. It is worth following this to explore what forms of gender transgression – in narrative or thematic terms – are to be found in the film to support such a reading. The answer, alas, is very few, and those which arise appear to emerge in a confused depiction of dominant female sexuality – in an early scene with her boyfriend, Tank Girl forces him to strip at gunpoint and, with her laser aimed at his genitals she demands that he 'salute'. His incapacity under threat mocks the pneumatic model of male sexuality – the moment is interrupted by the arrival of two of the commune's children in a perverse enactment of a Freudian primal scene (except these children are knowing). Tank Girl's journey is punctuated by opportunities to display a familiarity and knowing coolness about the pleasures of 'outlawed' modes of sexuality – masturbation, sadomasochism, lesbianism – as well as directly acknowledging male heterosexual fantasy. Later, Tank Girl kisses Jet Girl to pre-empt a repetition of sexual harassment at the hands of a Water and Power operative; she then enacts a double bluff by denying that this gesture was simply a comradely, asexual ruse, a 'come-on' for a homoerotic reading which is then forestalled by two of the Ripper characters metamorphosing into boyfriends in waiting.

At other times Tank Girl's 'femininity' takes on a direct association with a childlike set of responses (she is, after all, Tank *Girl*, not Tank Woman), where every victory over Kesslee prompts the cry 'I win!' – the loss of his arm after the Rippers' attack offers echoes of Captain Hook and obvious comparisons of Tank Girl as the fairly androgynous Peter Pan. 'Repaired' by means of a high-tech prosthesis, Kesslee becomes a character in a childhood nightmare, when comparisons with Freddy Krueger are hard to avoid – especially considering Talalay's previous projects. Female-specific experiences are woven into the narrative in such a way that we are reminded of contemporary meanings of femininity and their continuing currency in the 'real' world – the threat of sexual harassment to Jet Girl, the existence of a brothel in a post-apocalyptic world, where before Tank Girl rescues Sam from a would-be paedophile (another anachronistic moral note in the film) she is viewed trying on a series of stock sexualised feminine guises. Later in a carefully edited post-coital scene with the mutant roo, Booga, Tank Girl is seen wearing a pneumatic bra shaped like two missiles; while this image may be seen as ironic, indicating a performance of gender to denaturalise feminine/masculine associations,[29] at another narrative and visual level such meanings seem to be more fixed. This exaggeration of the female form in the enlargement of the breasts is both parody and reinforcement of sexual difference as 'naturalised'; even the transgressive possibilities of Tank Girl's bestial relationship with Booga are edged to the margins – as in the kiss with Jet Girl, other sexual possibilities are only seen to be toyed with.

The film, we would argue, actually fixes Tank Girl in the economy of gender by constantly engendering her position as hero(ine) in a way that a more conventional image, perhaps, does not. It has become a fairly established practice in contemporary feminist criticism of popular forms to counter earlier feminist critics who portrayed the female spectator as helplessly duped by the dominant meanings of the image as controlled by its 'sender'. Ien Ang, for instance, considers how readers negotiate their own pathways of resistance through unreconstructed images. Reviewing her analysis of audience responses to the *Dallas* character Sue Ellen and investigations of how female viewers negotiate the unreconstructed femininity of the character, Ang argues that identification with such characters *can* be challenging:

> The pleasure of such imaginary identification can be seen as a form of excess in some women's mode of experiencing everyday life in our culture: the act of surrendering to the melodramatic imagination may signify a recognition of the complexity and conflict fundamental to living in the modern world.[30]

Conventional femininity, in its ambiguous appeal to 'the natural', is more easily dismantled since it is always already based on contradictory ideological references. But what of the female image which invites us to contest conventional associations of femininity such as Tank Girl? Despite a 'feminist' rhetoric of control and power, the film exploits conventional Hollywood codes of spectatorship which encode the female body as site of display. Her clothes – tights, shorts and dungarees – are provocatively snipped and torn, but whereas the similar episode in the comic offered some critique of such structures of objectification, the film *Tank Girl* makes no attempt to indict the male viewer in the 'naturalness' of the dominant spectacularisation of the female body. For the heterosexual female viewer, the vicarious thrill of identification with a powerful female hero is undercut by the overall effect of a heroine who is empowered only to the extent that she is engendered as feminine. The 'new' transgressive feminine image remains dependent on the idea of gender which further entrenches difference, particularly when transgression is based on an ironic appropriation of the trappings of femininity combined with the most stereotypical of masculine and laddish attributes.

The narrative that is set in motion at the beginning of the film gives Tank Girl an emotional motivation for future actions, particularly her maternal responses to the abducted child, Sam. Her displacement in the martial masculine world of guns, tanks and weaponry is problematised by its overt (and predictably phallic) sexualisation. When she obtains her tank she caresses its gun to the theme of *Shaft* (1971): the scene promptly cuts to animation and her exclamation, 'My god, the sheer size of it!'; near the end of the film she points the tank's gun at two Water and Power workers, saying, 'Feeling inadequate?' Here is a woman with something bigger than a penis, in other words, a phallus: but she is symbolically situated in such a relation to it that we are constantly reminded of her 'lack' – right down to the regular groin shots, which seem to serve the dual purpose of displaying her masculine demeanour, but also her feminine disempowerment. 'Tank Girl' as realised on film is not without its contradictions and moments of transgressive 'resistance'. But the irony of the image needs a context that is easily displaced by its various readers, whether read against the grain or reappropriated for conventional sexual purposes. The unidimensional single story, the force of narrative closure and the dominant economy of spectatorial pleasure of Hollywood film are too rigid for the 'reader resistances' found with the comic form. Allied to the confusing and contradictory politics of femininity in a 'post-feminist' culture, there is a strong sense in which there is no real 'resistance' or 'challenge' which is not ultimately recuperated within the confines of a performance of female power for an orthodox male-defined spectator.

While the image of Tank Girl is powerful enough to be read in contradictory ways by various constituencies of readers, the *Diva* article concludes that Tank Girl is 'out there. Somewhere.' We can only conclude from her intertextual identity that Tank Girl is 'everywhere'; yet the constructions placed on this image confront a limit at the point of sexual transgression and gender disruption which, we suggest, always locates that space of confrontation 'elsewhere'.

Notes

1. In *Adult Comics: An Introduction* (London: Routledge, 1993), Roger Sabin looks back to their origins in the nineteenth century.
2. The term 'adult comic', however, tells us nothing about the average age group of the reader, but Sabin notes that 'the historically predominant target age range ... is sixteen to twenty-four', p. 3.
3. Barbara Klinger, 'Digressions at the cinema: commodification and reception in mass culture', in James Naremore and Patrick Brantlinger (eds), *Modernism and Mass Culture* (Bloomington: Indiana University Press, 1991), p. 132.
4. Tony Bennett and Janet Woollacott, *Bond and Beyond: The Political Career of a Popular Hero* (New York: Methuen, 1987), pp. 44–5. Quoted in Klinger, 'Digressions at the cinema', p. 21.
5. Sabin, *Adult Comics*, p. 210.
6. Alan Martin claims that 'We only set it in Australia because Jamie didn't want to draw any buildings.' Cited in Frank Wynne, *The Making of Tank Girl* (London: Titan Books, 1995), p. 11.
7. Particular references in one issue to 'Jane', 'Mike' and 'Mr Bishop' only made sense to us as a *Neighbours* reference because they coincided with our own knowledge of the soap in the late 1980s during a housebound and unemployed period of postgraduate life.

8. Sabin, *Adult Comics*, p. 108.
9. Ibid., p. 110.
10. Richard Reynolds, *Superheroes* (London: Batsford, 1992), p. 34.
11. Surprisingly, the promisingly titled *Women in the Comics* by Maurice Horn (New York: Chelsea House, 1977) bears this out. For further examples see Trina Robbins, *A Century of Women Cartoonists* (Northampton, MA: Kitchen Sink Press, 1993), especially ch. 7.
12. http://www.dcs.qmw.ad.uk/~bob/stuff/tg/stuff.html
13. Ibid.
14. Wynne, *The Making of Tank Girl*, p. 15.
15. Dale Spender, *Nattering on the Net* (Melbourne: Spinifex, 1995), p. 198.
16. 'The genius of Peter Duncan', *Hewlett and Martin's Tank Girl* (London: Penguin, 1990), p. 45.
17. Martin Barker, *Comics: Ideology, Power and the Critics* (Manchester: Manchester University Press, 1989), p. 258.
18. Louise Carolin, 'Comic strip tease', *Diva* (June/July 1995), p. 30.
19. Ibid., p. 33.
20. Ibid.
21. Ibid.
22. Written and illustrated by Diane DiMassa and published by Giant Ass Publishing, New Haven, Connecticut.
23. Carolin, 'Comic strip tease', p. 33.
24. The reference to Section 28 is mentioned in ibid.
25. Sabin, *Adult Comics*, p. 112.
26. Cited in Anita Chaudhuri, 'Tanks a lot', *Time Out*, 26 April–3 May 1995, p. 18.
27. In the film's 'Busby Berkeley' sequence, Tank Girl mimes heterosexual sex in the female-dominant position in a way which is closely reminiscent (if not identical) to one of Madonna's dance routines.
28. Camille Paglia, *Sex, Art and American Culture* (Harmondsworth: Penguin, 1992), p. 4.
29. See Judith Butler, *Gender Trouble* (New York: Routledge, 1990).
30. Ien Ang, *Living Room Wars: Rethinking Media Audiences for a Postmodern World* (London: Routledge, 1996), p. 188.

3

The Readers Feminism Doesn't See: Feminist Fans, Critics and Science Fiction

Helen Merrick

In late twentieth-century society, the images and language of Science Fiction (SF) have permeated every aspect of Western culture. The majority of the SF audience is composed of film and television viewers; however, literary SF still flourishes and maintains a number of dedicated readers who form part of the community or subculture known as SF fandom. The 'SF community' is generally taken to be made up of SF writers, fans, editors and publishers, who interact most visibly at SF conventions ('cons'), but also in various organisations, clubs and through 'fanzines' (amateur fan publications) and 'prozines' (such as *Locus*, which began as a fanzine, and the *New York Review of Science Fiction*). As Edward James writes,

> Since the late 1920s SF fandom – the body of enthusiastic and committed readers of SF – has had an appreciable and unique, if unmeasurable, impact on the evolution of SF, influencing writers, producing the genre's historians, bibliographers, and many of its best critics, and, above all, producing many of the writers themselves.[1]

The popularity of film and television SF has to some extent obscured the fact that in the last few decades an increasing number of feminist writers have utilised the medium of science fiction to express utopian and dystopian visions of the future, as well as critical interrogations of the contemporary gender order. Nonetheless, feminist science fiction is now a recognisable subgenre, where science fiction tropes and conventions are subverted and deconstructed to provide fertile ground for the articulation of feminist theories. Within the SF community, there are a substantial number of authors, fans and critics who identify themselves as feminist. Since the 1970s, feminist fan activity within SF has taken numerous forms, from writing feminist texts and publishing feminist fanzines to organising women-only spaces and feminist programming at conventions. More recently, a Net discussion group has been established to provide a forum for debate about contemporary feminist issues as well as SF texts.[2]

Despite the existence of such an innovative and flourishing field of feminist literature, SF is generally devalued by mainstream literary criticism as a 'low' mass market cultural product. Notwithstanding the influence of postmodernist deconstructions of hierarchies between high/low culture (and arguments claiming SF's special status as a literature of the postmodern), within the literary mainstream SF is still devalued as a pop culture product to be consumed by the masses rather than analysed by literary critics.[3] Traditionally seen as an inherently masculinist field, feminist SF remains a marginalised presence even in feminist criticism. Apart from an occasional special issue in mainstream literary/cultural journals, the criticism of feminist SF is confined largely to the SF field, and still remains outside the central concerns of feminist literary criticism.[4] Within the science fiction field, a specialised feminist SF literary criticism has developed, producing what could be seen as a 'canon' of texts. Critics refer to a 'tradition' of feminist utopian writing from the 1970s, exemplified by works such as Ursula Le Guin's *The Dispossessed* (1974), Joanna Russ' *The Female Man* (1975), Marge Piercy's *Woman on the Edge of Time* (1976), Suzy McKee Charnas' *Motherlines* (1978) and Sally Miller Gearhart's *The Wanderground* (1979).[5] These texts are often counterposed to the predominantly dystopian visions of the 1980s, usually epitomised by Margaret Atwood's *The Handmaid's Tale* (1986).

While marginalised from the literary mainstream, feminist SF criticism has remained textually focused, based on a literary critical model and rarely drawing on other feminist theoretical projects, such as feminist film theory or cultural studies. Unlike its media counterpart, studies of literary SF have neglected the processes of production and reception of the text, a rather surprising omission for a genre which has been so closely associated with and even shaped by its unique group of fans.[6] Despite the importance of fans to the SF community, their influence and even presence is at best marginal in most critical accounts, even though the experiences of female and feminist fans have been an integral part of the development of feminist SF.

In this article, I shall examine some of the developments in cultural studies approaches to audience analysis which could provide a preliminary model for the study of feminist SF fandom. I argue that the analysis of feminist SF should draw on cultural theories to consider the readings and activities of that specialised audience, the SF fan. A variety of theoretical models have sought to explain the nature of the interaction between readers and texts. Importantly, the critics who provide these descriptions are themselves 'readers': however, the process of observation and interpretation which distinguishes critics' readings suggests that they have a different relationship to the text than that of the readers they analyse. The act of criticism authorises specific types of reading which must be elucidated by the critic in order to provide the general reader with a 'correct' path to follow. The act of criticism itself limits the active production of meanings from a text by providing a specific reading that becomes reified as an authorised, specialised and informed mode of reading, and which can insist that certain meanings are inherent to the text.

In recent literary theory, there have been significant changes in the way the reader–text relationship has been conceptualised. The trend has been towards 'reader-response' theories that acknowledge a level of independence in the reading of a text, including, for example, theories about gendered reading positions. Studies of classic, canonical literature tend to work on the model of an individual reader, yet studies of genre fiction tend to concentrate more on 'audiences' and how groups of people respond to specific styles of text. A good example of the 'audience' approach is Janice Radway's *Reading the Romance* (1987), which provided a feminist analysis of a female 'community' of Harlequin romance novel readers. Radway broadened the focus from a consideration of reader–text relationships to an examination of a combination of textual and extratextual analyses such as ethnographic accounts of the 'audience', psychoanalytic interpretations and analysis of the mass-market romance industry.

Ethnographic surveys of audiences have become staples of popular culture studies, and the emphasis on group 'readings' would seem to be a more suitable approach to fandom than the focus on the individual reader offered by literary criticism. As Lisa Lewis points out, fans are the most 'visible and identifiable of audiences', and yet they have been overlooked by scholars, largely due to the 'propensity to treat media audiences as passive and controlled'.[7] Recent work focusing on fans as a specialised audience deal mostly with the popular mass media, with surprisingly little work done on literary SF fandom.[8] However, one still has to be careful in classifying audiences, readers and fan communities. While fans seem to provide a ready-made constituency, a self-identified 'audience', they do not necessarily represent the majority of SF readers. In fact, their level of familiarity and knowledge of the field differentiate them from the general audience of genre/popular fiction readers. Thus within cultural studies, fans represent a very particular and unique audience, whose readings and uses of texts cannot necessarily be presented as 'typical' in formulating theories of how SF is consumed by a mass audience.

Cultural studies approaches to the mass media have proliferated since the 1970s, developing a number of theories of audiences, and, more recently, of fans and fandom. An important cultural critic often cited in studies of SF is Michel de Certeau, whose *The Practice of Everyday Life* (1984) constructed models of the popular and 'everyday' that recognised more agency in the practice of consumption and reading than had previously been acknowledged. De Certeau criticised the conventional view of mass culture as necessarily conservative and dictatorial. He held that the prevailing view that 'the public is moulded by the products imposed on it', was based on the incorrect assumption that 'consumerism is essentially passive'.[9] Such theories were based on a conception of writing/reading analogous to the production–consumption binary, where 'reading' was seen to 'constitute the maximal development of the passivity assumed to characterise the consumer, who is conceived of as a voyeur'. In contrast, de Certeau characterised reading as a 'silent production', as an 'art which is anything but passive'.[10] One of the images that de Certeau used to describe the way consumers or readers of popular culture engage in an active form of production was that of 'poaching': 'everyday life invents itself by *poaching* in countless ways on the property of others'.[11]

This metaphor seems particularly appropriate to both literary and mass media SF, where poaching can take the form of the production of new texts such as fanzines. In Henry Jenkins' study, mass media SF fans are described as 'textual poachers' who transform and rewrite the texts provided by TV shows, and in the process engage with the texts as active participants in a mass cultural formation, long seen as a didactic and one-way process of reception or consumption.[12] The activity of fans mediates against the myth of passivity among mass market audiences, and as Patrick Parrinder notes, fandom 'is incompatible with simply reading for consumption'.[13] As Jenkins observes, it is ironic that

> before Cultural Studies began to research fan culture, fans were dismissed as atypical of the media audience because of their obsessiveness and extreme passivity; now that ethnographic accounts of fan culture are beginning to challenge those assumptions, fans are dismissed as atypical of the media audience because of their activity and resistance.[14]

From a cultural studies perspective, fans represent a very particular and unique audience, whose readings and uses of texts cannot necessarily be used in formulating theories of how SF is read or viewed by a general audience. Yet fans often do impact on the production of the primary text, especially in the SF community, with its tradition of close contact between fans, writers, editors and publishers. Thus fans are often an important factor in the production of the source, and fandom should therefore be studied as a culture in and of itself.

In addition to the problem of situating the fan in the text/audience nexus is the question of the relationship between the scholar and fan – between observer and observed. In the

SF community in particular there exists a tradition of hostility between fans and academic critics. Certainly in the period before SF critical journals were established, studies of SF from outside the community were often based on ignorance and contempt of the field, in an era when literary criticism was only deemed appropriate for an elite canon of texts of 'great literature'. David Hartwell also suggests that

> one aspect of the antipathy in fandom to the growing attention that literary critics and academics have been paying to SF in the last decade or so is that such attention from outside the field must interfere with fandom's demand upon the writers for primary consideration. This is the first substantial challenge to the primacy and authority of fandom in the history of the field.[15]

Even though SF criticism is now a well-established field with its own academic specialists, the *positioning* of the critic in relation to the reader or fan (and the associated questions of hierarchy and authority) has been the subject of little interrogation. While much recent feminist SF criticism acknowledges the academic commentator's identity as both fan and critic, there is no examination of how the critic's specific reading is privileged over all other readings, or what authorises the act of interpretation when carried out by a critic rather than a fan. These questions are brought to the fore when the object of study is not the text, but the users of the text.

The notion of the critic as objective observer has largely been rejected by most feminist and cultural theorists; instead there is recognition of a central predicament of ethnography: 'The fact that it is always caught up in the invention, not the representation of cultures.'[16] Despite the apparent abandonment of the possibility of an objective, removed position from which to observe, there remains an attachment to the idea of critics/scholars as being separate from the culture they observe, privileged by superior, 'outside' knowledge and the methodologies which enable them to translate the subject into appropriate academic language. In other words, it is assumed that critics still need to maintain distance from their subject, or risk becoming too close to, or involved in the culture under scrutiny, rendering their account partial, biased and thus uncritical. For example, when Lawrence Grossberg wanted to teach university classes on rock music, colleagues argued that he was not the 'appropriate person' to teach the class as he was a fan. 'While I disagreed with their implicit assumption that fans could not have any critical distance, I was fascinated by their insight that, somehow, being a fan entails a very different relationship to culture, a relationship which seems only to exist in the realm of popular culture.'[17] In opposition to this view, in the realm of feminist and post-colonial studies during the 1990s there has been a strong tendency towards the view that *only* the members of a particular culture (mediated by gender, race, class) can write about their culture or adopt the authority to speak about and thus for members of a community.[18]

The relationship between the fan and source is seen to be excessive because popular culture texts are not generally regarded as meriting such intense scrutiny. Jenkins suggests that the negative stereotypical image of the fan may be related to 'anxieties about the violation of dominant cultural hierarchies', where fan cultures transgress these boundaries, 'treating popular texts as if they merited the same degree of attention and appreciation as canonical texts'.[19]

Interestingly, a number of cultural critics have commented on similarities between fans and academics. Patrick Parrinder has argued that becoming a fan involves 'initiation into an unofficial field of knowledge' which has parallels with the 'official field of orthodox literary knowledge'.[20] Joli Jensen notes the parallel between the fans' obsessions and the scholars' devotion to their research interests, which is obscured due to 'a system of bias which debases fans and elevates scholars even though they engage in virtually the same kinds of activities'.[21] Similarly, Jenkins points to the potential for fans to function as critics – to employ those practices usually reserved for an educated elite: 'Within the realm of popular culture, fans are the true experts; they constitute a competing educational elite, albeit one without official recognition or social power.'[22]

Studies of popular culture consumption would also suggest that SF fans and academics/critics have more in common than the 'general' consumer of popular fiction. Both have a commitment to engaged, critical and interpretative consumption of texts – interpretative in the sense that engagement with the text goes beyond the initial reading to verbal or written discussion of the text with others. Critics publish their interpretations, fans discuss them in zines, cons and increasingly through Internet discussion groups: the process of interpretation is for both an avenue for making statements about their own identity and positioning within their respective communities, for both it is a site of pleasure (and a certain amount of power). The suggestion of similarities between fans and critics has interesting implications for studies where the subject is fan culture itself. Given that current ethnographic studies hold participation to be as important as observation, thus dissolving to some extent the boundary between ethnography and community, we should ask what distinguishes the accounts of critics as opposed to fans.

Critics offer a number of readings when writing about audiences or fans; first they provide an account of the fans' activities and usually some analysis of what these activities 'mean' both to the fans themselves and in terms of theories about texts and audiences in popular culture. Critics may also provide their own interpretations of the primary texts of the fandom, which are often inherently privileged over the fans' own 'readings' as deciphered through the observation of the critic. For example, Radway's account of female readers of romance also includes her own critical accounts of the texts which make apparent their 'inherent' meaning and its subconscious effect on the (unaware) reader. Following cultural critics like Constance Penley and Henry Jenkins, I would argue that critical readings of texts have a place in audience studies, but that is to show that there are a multiplicity of reading positions available, rather than to provide a standard against which 'inferior' readings are measured.

In his work on *Star Trek* fans, Jenkins suggests the possibility of reconciling critical work on texts, institutional analyses of their production and audience research of reception contexts, by reading the text from the specific perspective of particular audiences and creating analyses in dialogue with these reception communities.[23] Stating his own identity to be that of both fan and academic, Jenkins sees his critical account as existing in a 'constant movement between these two levels of understanding which are not necessarily in conflict but are also not necessarily in perfect alignment'. However, he goes on to note the risk of over-identification with the research subject, citing David Sholle's warning that '[t]here is a danger of taking up the standpoint of a fan and thus confusing one's own stance with that of the subject being studied'.[24]

While Jenkins acknowledges the importance of his fan identity and is critical of earlier academic approaches which judged but did not converse with the fan community, and as a result often 'transformed fandom into a projection of their own personal fears, anxieties, and fantasies about the dangers of mass culture',[25] there remains a certain disparity between academic and fan which is unresolved. While Jenkins denies many of the traditional trappings of authority endowed in the academic persona, he does not address what it is that produces (or maintains) the 'distance' between ethnographer and subject, especially if they are both members of the same community. The study of female *Star Trek* fans by Camille Bacon-Smith approaches the problem of positioning differently, but produces no better a resolution. One of her overriding concerns is to avoid 'intruding' into or misreading the fan community she describes, while acknowledging the impossibility of undertaking such study until she is a member of the community. Her identity as observer remains problematic, as she constantly reinscribes herself as an 'outsider' through constant use of the term 'ethnographer' to refer to herself at conventions and even when transcribing interviews and conversations. So while at the experiential level Bacon-Smith becomes (an increasingly accepted) member of the community, her writing positions her as a nameless outsider/observer who is thus granted the authority and distance to write about the experiences of women, including herself. Bacon-Smith's account is structured as an almost epic quest to the 'heart' of this fandom, an essential secret that can only be revealed as she is allowed into the inner sanctum and 'discovers' that the motivation of the fan's creativity is pain and vulnerability. Yet as Jenkins points out, such experiences are not confined to fans, and certainly do not explain their involvement in creating slash fiction (homoerotic stories about popular SF characters such as Spock and Kirk) and art, nor does it reflect the extent to which 'poaching' might be a site of female strength and subversion.[26]

In contrast, Constance Penley's accounts of female slash fandom not only present a very different view of the women involved, but clearly address the problem of her own positioning as both fan and critic. Penley signals the difference between her analysis of slash fandom and Bacon-Smith's account by stating that she is not interested in 'uncovering and describing yet another "subculture" for the sake of adding it to a now almost canonical group of subcultures'.[27] Rather, she focuses on the insights that arise from her personal observations and interaction with this group of women, and describes how this encounter has changed her way of thinking about issues such as women and pornography, popular pleasure, the social and psychological role of fantasy, and the popular reception of feminism. Unlike Bacon-Smith, Penley does not regard herself as an analytical void waiting to be filled up or enlightened by what is 'revealed' to her by the fans; she has specific interests and questions that result from her work as cultural critic which are transformed, confirmed or rejected through her encounter. Penley's intention in writing about this fan culture is not to document their 'real' selves, motives and desires, but to initiate further speculation about *possible* interactions between women, popular culture and feminism.

The presence of a critical agenda informing Penley's analysis does not, however, override her observations; often her interaction with fandom has forced a reassessment of her theoretical assumptions. For example, Penley's feminism leads her to identify many of the fans' views and sentiments as 'feminist', yet she recognises that most do not see themselves as feminists or speak from a consciously feminist position – their primary identification remains that of a fan. Penley argues that such research teaches us valuable lessons about the study of feminism and popular culture. While Penley recognises that she and other commentators would love to claim this fandom as an 'exemplary case' of female appropriation of and resistance to mass-produced culture, these fans do not feel they can speak as feminists. Penley writes,

> Fandom, the various popular ideologies of abuse and self-help, and New Age philosophies are seen as far more relevant to their needs and desires than what they perceive as a middle class feminism that disdains popular culture and believes that pornography degrades women.[28]

One respondent to Penley's paper commented that, as a critic, she explicitly aligned herself with the fans and allowed herself 'no privileged insight into the original text'.[29] Penley replied that while she had learnt much from identifying as a fan, much of her knowledge came from observing her distance from the fans in terms of her feminism and also the class difference she attributes to her professional training. Fans did not so much disagree with her interpretations of slash culture, as with the language and method of her presentation: 'In fact, [the fans] have more difficulty with what they call my tendency to "intellectualise" than they do with my being an avowed feminist.'[30] Penley suggests that fans also disliked the tendency to generalisation which is a necessary part of any critical or theoretical project, as they wanted to retain the individuality and specificity of every member.

While these studies of mass media fan culture provide useful insights for a study of literary SF fandom, many of the distinctions Penley describes between herself and *Star Trek* fans do not hold for explicitly feminist SF fandom. In the US, for example, there has been a group of overtly feminist fans writing about a body of feminist texts and producing critical (rather than fictional) material. Fanzines such as *Janus*, *Aurora* and *The Witch and the Chameleon* situated not only the SF texts, but also fandom in both the socio-historical SF context and also broader socio-political movements such as feminism, civil and gay rights. Audience and fan studies are vital to a broader cultural study of feminist SF, not least because the significance of the genre lies in its extratextual dimensions, such as fan readings, zines, cons and the close interaction between publishers, editors, authors and audience that epitomises the 'SF community'. There is also a need for a cultural history of feminism and SF, rather than just a literary history or construction of a tradition which often privileges feminist utopian writings over the broader SF field and the contexts within which feminist SF, and critical responses to it, are produced.

A couple of recent examples from the SF community serve to underline the importance of undertaking such a cultural history. In an article, 'The women SF doesn't see', SF author Connie Willis argues that earlier female writers who were an essential part of the development of feminist SF have been neglected and even dismissed because of critics' fairly rigid definitions of feminism.[31] Critics have neglected the influence of early female writers such as Judith Merril, Zenna Henderson and Margaret St. Clair – writing in the 1940s and 1950s – who in their writing and their mere presence in the field paved the way for later feminist writers. Similarly, a prominent feminist fan, Jeanne Gomoll, has recounted how her experiences of fandom are being rewritten in retrospective panels on 1970s fandom which omit any reference to feminist activity and therefore obscure the contribution of such fans to the development of feminist SF.[32] This further contributes to the reactionary view (that many have observed in the cyberpunk movement) that the 1970s was a 'boring decade' in SF where nothing of any significance occurred.

A cultural study of feminist SF encompassing the experiences of fans could shed new light on a number of 'truisms' of SF criticism. One SF myth that could be re-examined with reference to a history of feminist fans is that there are no women in the genre. A common assumption remains that SF was (and is) almost totally male-dominated, with only the occasional, exceptional female writer, and even fewer female readers before the 1960s. Many accounts suggest that the number of female fans was so small as to be insignificant, and even more tellingly, that those that did exist were secondary fans – the wives, girlfriends, female relatives of male fans. The fan historian Harry Warner has written that in the 1940s there were 'no independent girl-type fans'.[33] The key word here is independent, the implication being that connection with a male delegitimated the female fan identity – she was only involved because of male influence. In retrospect, this is a rather fallacious argument – now that there are many more women involved in fandom, many still make significant partnerships within the community precisely because of the shared interests and commitments. There is evidence of the existence of female fans from the very beginning of fandom in the 1930s and 1940s, appearing in the occasional letters sent by women to magazines such as *Astounding*. A coherent account that brought together all the scattered references and sources testifying to the presence of female fans would counter the arguments which continue to assert the absence of women as readers and fans of SF before the 1960s.

In general accounts of fandom, the absence of women is taken as an obvious fact, with the unspoken assumption that women's lack of interest was the cause. There is very seldom any acknowledgement that there were definite disincentives to women and opposition to female fans in the community at large. In magazines such as *Astounding* in the 1930s, letters from women often drew very antagonistic responses from men (including a renowned author) and one woman in particular detailed the misgivings she experienced while deciding whether or not to make her presence visible.[34]

Individual opposition to female fans was often expressed in terms of the phallocentric dichotomy assigning women to nature and men to science. Many male fans' letters expressed the belief that allowing women into SF (as readers or characters) was in fact a ploy to bring love interests and sex into SF – as if it was only through these themes that women could have any kind of relationship with science and thus SF. Although the question of 'women and SF' was debated since the SF fan community emerged, until the late 1960s the issue was really 'sex and SF' – this conflation of women and sex being rarely challenged until the rise of feminist critiques during the 1970s.

Other issues which could be productively re-examined with the benefit of a history of female fans include the impetus for their increasing numbers, and how the arrival or 'invasion' of female fans has been viewed by the wider SF community. In many accounts, *Star Trek* is seen as one of the primary motivations for female involvement in SF, which again obscures the possibility of women readers of earlier SF, and assigns women to a sphere of SF fandom that is often devalued, where the attraction apparently lies in the 'love interest' created between Spock and Kirk. While *Star Trek* undoubtedly popularised SF among a previously unconverted audience, it is unlikely that this interest always translated to full fan activity; in addition, many of those who did enter fandom through *Star Trek* created a separate fandom with its own identity and writers. Many feminist SF authors claim their earliest experiences of SF were of reading the pulp magazines. Thus the increase in female authors that is commonly thought to have inspired increasing numbers of female fans was, in most cases, based on an immersion in the more 'traditional' SF works. In most accounts of the increase in women fans, little agency is given to the fans themselves. Many critics consider that the climate of SF production has changed and become 'softer' and thus proved more attractive to women. Little emphasis is put on the efforts that female fans themselves made to change the environment of the SF community – for example, the efforts by Susan Wood and others in organising women spaces at cons, starting panels on women and SF, and founding feminist zines and a women-only Amateur Publishing Association (APA).[35]

Feminist SF represents an important site of interaction between feminism, science and culture which is extremely significant in light of the continuing feminist critiques of the gendered relations of science and technology. In the field of feminist science theory, a number of critics such as Donna Haraway and Hilary Rose have valorised feminist SF for its potential contribution to a feminist politics on science and technology.[36] The feminist interventions into the traditionally masculinist areas of SF and science represented by feminist SF are not played out solely on a textual level. Beyond each author's individual text are the cultural ramifications for female readers gaining access (if only fictionally) to science and technology, and of SF fans drawing from (and providing) the impetus of feminist SF to create a feminist space within fandom which changes their community.

I believe that female fans are an integral part of the construction of 'feminist SF' which has thus far mostly been confined to the academic study of literary texts. The development of a specialised feminist SF criticism has established various groupings and divisions between feminist, feminised, women's and 'domestic' SF, in effect a process of internal canon formation leading to a critical concentration on certain texts at the expense of a consideration of the reading experiences of fans or general female SF readers. A study of the interaction of feminism with SF should not be confined to critical analyses of the 'feminist' characteristics of the texts alone. Such an approach obscures one of the most significant aspects of feminist SF – that is, the way the texts are utilised by readers and fans to provide a forum for feminist organisation, action and debate.

Notes

1. Edward James, *Science Fiction in the Twentieth Century* (Oxford: Oxford University Press, 1994), p. 130.
2. The Internet discussion group address is kept private, as admission is by invitation only.
3. See, for example, Roger Luckhurst's argument that postmodernist critics of SF who claim to erase the high/low cultural divide ultimately always reinscribe this border, 'Border policing: postmodernism and science fiction', *Science Fiction Studies* 18, 3 (1991), pp. 358–66.
4. A fact highlighted in the work of Marleen S. Barr, who suggests quite radical measures in order to deal with this problem (stemming from frustration, one feels, after a decade's critical work unacknowledged by the feminist mainstream). See, for example, Marleen S. Barr, *Feminist Fabulation: Space/Postmodern Fiction* (Iowa City: University of Iowa Press, 1992) and *Lost in Space: Probing Feminist Science Fiction and Beyond* (Chapel Hill: North Carolina University Press, 1993).
5. Joanna Russ' seminal article, 'Recent feminist utopias', in Marleen S. Barr (ed.), *Future Females: A Critical Anthology* (Bowling Green: Bowling Green State University Press, 1981), pp. 71–85, also discusses: Monique Wittig, *Les Guérillères*; Marion Zimmer Bradley, *The Shattered Chain*; Samuel Delany, *Triton*; James Tiptree Jr (aka Alice Sheldon), 'Houston, Houston, do you read?' and 'Your faces, O my sisters! Your faces filled of light!'.

6. See, for example, David Hartwell, *Age of Wonders: Exploring the World of Science Fiction* (New York, Walker, 1984), who comments that fans 'play a central and crucial role in making the SF field what it is. Without fandom, SF might never have established itself as a genre ... The activities of fans have kept it alive and vigorous', p. 158.

7. Lisa A. Lewis, 'Introduction', in Lewis (ed.), *The Adoring Audience: Fan Culture and Popular Media* (London: Routledge, 1992), p. 1.

8. Most cultural studies of SF fandom focus on *Star Trek*, particularly the activities of the female slash zine writers, which now boasts a long list of detailed studies. In the Lewis collection for example, there is only one article about SF fandom, and it is about the specific activity of 'filking', see Henry Jenkins, '"Strangers no more, we sing": filking and the social construction of the science fiction fan community', in Lewis, *Adoring Audience*, pp. 208–36.

9. Michel de Certeau, *The Practice of Everyday Life*, trans. Steven F. Rendall (Berkeley: University of California Press, 1984), p. 167.

10. Ibid., pp. xxi–xxii.

11. Ibid., p. xii.

12. Henry Jenkins, *Textual Poachers: Television Fans and Participatory Culture* (London: Routledge, 1992). Jenkins distinguishes between his use and de Certeau's formulation, in that while de Certeau describes solitary readers whose 'poaching' serves only their own interests, fan reading is a social process and fandom does not preserve the radical separation between readers and writers suggested by de Certeau, pp. 44–5.

13. Patrick Parrinder, *Science Fiction: Its Criticism and Teaching* (London: Methuen, 1980), p. 41.

14. Jenkins, *Textual Poachers*, p. 287.

15. David Hartwell, *Age of Wonders: Exploring the World of Science Fiction* (New York: Walker, 1984), pp. 168–9.

16. James Clifford, 'Introduction: partial truths', in James Clifford and George E. Marcus (eds), *Writing Culture: The Poetics and Politics of Ethnography* (Berkeley: University of California Press, 1986), p. 2.

17. Lawrence Grossberg, 'Is there a fan in the house?: the affective sensibility of fandom', in Lewis (ed.), *Adoring Audience*, p. 50.
18. See, for example, Judith Roof and Robyn Wiegman (eds), *Who Can Speak? Authority and Critical Identity* (Urbana: University of Illinois Press, 1991).
19. Jenkins, *Textual Poachers*, p. 17.
20. Parrinder, *Science Fiction*, p. 41.
21. Lewis, 'Introduction', *Adoring Audience*, p. 2.
22. Jenkins, *Textual Poachers*, p. 86.
23. Henry Jenkins and John Tulloch, *Science Fiction Audiences: Watching Doctor Who and Star Trek* (London: Routledge, 1995), p. 239.
24. Jenkins, *Textual Poachers*, pp. 5–6.
25. Ibid., p. 6.
26. See Jenkins and Tulloch, *Science Fiction Audiences*, p. 203.
27. Constance Penley, 'Feminism, psychoanalysis and the study of popular culture', in Lawrence Grossberg et al. (eds), *Cultural Studies* (London: Routledge, 1992), p. 500. See also Penley, 'Brownian motion: women, tactics and technology', in C. Penley and A. Ross (eds), *Technoculture* (Minneapolis: University of Minnesota Press, 1990), pp. 135–61.
28. Penley, 'Feminism', p. 492. Unlike Bacon-Smith, who seems to follow the fans in rejecting a feminist framework for her work, Penley employs a feminist analysis of their texts and production. She makes plain, however, that this is her own interpretation, not that of the fans, one that is not therefore more correct, but different precisely because she is speaking and writing from a different identificatory position.
29. John Fiske in discussion of Penley, 'Feminism', p. 495.
30. Penley, 'Feminism', p. 496.
31. Connie Willis, 'Guest editorial: the women SF doesn't see', *Asimov's SF Magazine* 16, 11 (October 1992), pp. 4–8.
32. Jeanne Gomoll, 'An open letter to Joanna Russ', *Aurora* 10, 1 (1986–7), pp. 7–10.
33. Harry Warner Jr, *All Our Yesterdays: An Informal History of SF Fandom in the Forties* (Chicago: Advent, 1969), p. 26. Here he also mentions that by 1948 a Tucker survey

showed 11 per cent of fans to be female – not an insignificant number. Warner also comments that in general it is very difficult to estimate the number of fans, and that 'there must have been large numbers of fans not visible' – and female fans would have been much more likely than male fans to be invisible, p. 24.

34. I am extremely grateful to Justine Larbelestier for providing me with these details from her (as yet unpublished) PhD research.

35. Amateur Publishing Associations (APAs) are another fan publishing activity. They have a limited mailing list, generally under 30 people; members send contributions to a coordinator, who collates them and mails the whole (often called apazine) to each member. APA contributions are usually in the form of a personal letter, and many talk about going to cons, or describe their current reading. Members also include comments in reply to every other member's piece in the last 'issue'. The result is a very personalised conversation with up to 20 or 30 people, often from different countries. Some examples include TWP (The Women's Periodical) set up in Britain for women only, AWA (A Women's APA) in the US, which has been women-only at various stages, and BWA (The 'B' Women's APA, that is, a second Women's APA), also set up in the US and women-only. All of these APAs have had members in the US, UK, Europe and Australia.

36. Donna Haraway, 'A manifesto for cyborgs: science, technology and socialist feminism in the 1980s', in Linda J. Nicholson (ed.), *Feminism/Postmodernism* (London: Routledge, 1990), pp. 190–233; Hilary Rose, *Love, Power and Knowledge: Towards a Feminist Transformation of the Sciences* (Cambridge: Polity Press, 1994).

4

There's No Accounting for Taste: Exploitation Cinema and the Limits of Film Theory

Paul Watson

> The easiest, and so the most frequent and most spectacular
> way to 'shock the bourgeois' ... is done by conferring aesthetic
> status on objects or ways of representing them that are
> excluded by the dominant aesthetic of the time.[1]
>
> Pierre Bourdieu

Most theoretically and historically informed accounts of the
cinema exclude from their considerations the complex
interaction of historical, social and economic discourses at play
in the term 'exploitation cinema'. Inasmuch as there has been
discussion of exploitation cinema at all, then it has tended to
be overwhelmingly centred on two key areas.

First, with the rapid ossification of film theory and
historiography (prematurely) enshrined in academic discourse,
exploitation cinema, which could not readily be tailored to
fit either the dominant historiographic paradigm of cinema
or the requirements of educational curricula, was ostracised
to the pages of cinephile magazines and books.[2] But although
cinephilic discourse has been successful in at least illuminating
the stygian world of exploitation, and instrumental in the
documentation of many long-forgotten films, it has
simultaneously served to marginalise it from the academy's
gaze: if cinephiles were documenting the history of exploitation
then there was little need for the academy to write it into film
history. And this is the basic paradox of exploitation cinema:
it is precisely its ability to resist and escape established networks
of theoretical and historical discourse that makes it of
fundamental interest and importance to those discourses,

even as that same elusive quality condemns it to remain in the province of cinephilia. Ironically, this inadvertent tendency to confine exploitation to the margins of critical debate in the very act of investigating it has recently extended to the academy itself. In his useful article, 'Trashing the academy', Jeffrey Sconce locates exploitation film as a central element in what he calls 'paracinema' – the name is significant. Sconce argues that paracinema is 'a most elastic textual category' and is 'less a distinct group of films than a particular reading protocol, a counter aesthetic turned sub-cultural sensibility devoted to all manner of cultural detritus'.[3]

Here lies the second major approach to exploitation: its postmodern recuperation as trash and cult cinema. Sconce notes that 'the caustic rhetoric of paracinema suggests a pitched battle between a guerilla band of cult viewers and an elite cadre of would-be taste makers. Certainly, the paracinematic audience likes to see itself as a disruptive force in the cultural and intellectual marketplace.'[4] There is an implicit blindspot here. Such a calculated negation of Hollywood cinema suggests that exploitation film exists beyond or outside of mainstream culture. The cultivation of 'a counter-cinema from the dregs of exploitation films' and the *a fortiori* positioning of the paracinematic writer as 'explicitly ... in opposition to Hollywood and the mainstream US culture it represents' belies the fact that exploitation cinema has to a large extent always gone hand in hand with precisely that cultural mainstream. And its recuperation as a kind of postmodern avant-garde merely serves further to bury its true significance in the margins and footnotes of our theories. Indeed, while avoiding the danger of stripping it of all historical specificity, I want to suggest that if the concept of exploitation is to be retained today, then its significance relates not to the realms of the paracinema, but rather to the fundamental aesthetic and economic axioms by which Hollywood operates.

It is here that we confront the fundamental theoretical, not to mention political, problem of exploitation. For the instant one thinks of exploitation as a form of film, its neglect is both remarkable and predictable. It is remarkable insofar as the exploitation aesthetic not only predated the advent of cinema, but was also to a large extent integral to its development. In nineteenth-century optical technologies, the immediate precursors to the cinematic apparatus, lay the quiddity of an exploitation aesthetic which would be fully realised in its synthesis with cinematic technologies. By an ironic inversion, cinema might be thought of as an avatar of exploitation. If one accepts this ironic turn in the relationship of cinema to exploitation, then the neglect of exploitation film is only too predictable. For one is impelled to conclude that cinema cannot be addressed without also addressing its relation to exploitation, and that addressing the nature of exploitation not only brings one face to face with the pre-history of cinema, but challenges, and even displaces, certain axioms of film theory and film study.

This claim appears to be extraordinary, but is in fact entirely predictable when one takes into account the role of taste and the effect of aesthetic discrimination. For from its first moments Film Studies' theories and canons have been bound up with an economy of taste which influences questions not only of how to approach cinema, but questions of what cinema to approach in the first instance. Dominant notions of cinematic aesthetics have been installed and defended on the basis of the assumed excellence of taste of a relative few privileged journalists and critics, appealing to canons and principles of art in general. This is not to say that there haven't been shifts in the cinematic canon, or that those canons are uncontested, but that those shifts and contests are themselves tied to shifts in taste which have tended overwhelmingly to exclude exploitation. Of course, a case can be made that critical and academic appreciation is of little relevance to exploitation film practice and that commercial success is the only yardstick of any consequence. But although in one sense this is true, such a claim masks as much as it reveals. Despite its absence of artistic pretention, exploitation cinema has much to offer precisely those canons of film and film theory which continue to reject it on aesthetic grounds. Besides, just because exploitation films declare no explicit artistic agenda doesn't mean that they shouldn't be considered alongside forms of cinema that do. The notion that the 'taste' of an educated 'elite' with refined sensibilities constitutes the litmus test of film appreciation is just one instance of a complex set of socio-cultural propositions determined by equally diverse ideological and economic factors that conspire to regulate both what is on and what is off the critical agenda.

The most important account of the cultural logic of taste is provided by Pierre Bourdieu's *Distinction*. In his study of French bourgeois culture Bourdieu argues that class segments define themselves as distinct from one another by virtue of contrasting aesthetic judgements and different attitudes towards art and beauty. He writes that 'taste classifies, and it classifies the classifier. Social subjects, classified by their classifications, distinguish themselves by the distinctions they make, between the beautiful and the ugly, the distinguished and the vulgar, in which their position in the objective classifications is exposed or betrayed.'[5] For Bourdieu the cultural consumption of aesthetics and the social economy of taste behind that process are predisposed to 'fulfil a social function of legitimating social differences'.[6] Clearly, taste is thus not simply a question of personal choice divorced from ideological or economic determinants, but is, on the contrary, fundamentally a political issue. As Bourdieu notes, at stake in every struggle over art and aesthetics is 'also the imposition of an art of living, that is, the transmutation of an arbitrary way of living into the legitimate way of life which casts every other way of living into arbitrariness'.[7] In this way, tastes are the 'practical affirmation of an inevitable difference',[8] inevitable not in a pre-ordained sense, but in the sense that we are forced to judge: there is no escape from the necessity to make judgements in any specific case. Yet, with the epistemological shift to postmodernism, we have few grounds available on which to base those judgements which are not aesthetic in origin. And it is no accident that the justification of taste, and in particular the dominant taste, is an entirely negative process. That is, tastes are asserted and defended by the refusal of other tastes. Bourdieu writes that 'in matters of taste, more than anywhere else, all determination is negation'. Somewhat ironically, therefore, he concludes that 'tastes are perhaps first and foremost distastes, disgust provoked by horror of visceral intolerance ("sick-making") of the tastes of others'.[9]

One stultifying result of the system of aesthetic discrimination that underpins notions of cultural distinction is that it tends to exclude, or at least marginalise, most of what this chapter is concerned with on the grounds that it is futile and unworthy of critical attention. In *Incredibly Strange Films*, one of the few books that tackles the question of exploitation cinema, Vale and Juno make the point that the concept of 'good taste' 'functions as a filter to block out entire areas of experience judged – and damned – as unworthy of investigation'.[10] While this appears to be an exaggerated claim, Bourdieu suggests that such filters are entirely predictable, inevitable by-products of the logic of taste. Since an aversion to different aesthetics is one of the strongest barriers between the classes, it is not surprising that 'the most intolerable thing for those who regard themselves as the possessors of legitimate culture is the reuniting of tastes that taste dictates shall be separated'.[11] The main point here is that the notions of 'pure taste' and legitimate culture can only be defined in relation to precisely what they are not. This has historically tended to lead to the excision of all that does not fit the definition of 'taste' from the space of cultural critique and social theory. Bourdieu notes that:

> 'Pure taste' and the aesthetics which provide its theory are founded on a refusal of 'impure' taste and of *aisthesis* (sensation), the simple, primitive form of pleasure of the senses, as in what Kant calls 'the taste of the tongue, the palate and the throat', a surrender to immediate sensation which in another order looks like imprudence.[12]

This leads Bourdieu to conclude that the whole language of aesthetics 'is contained in a fundamental refusal of the *facile*; that "pure taste", purely negative in its essence, is based on the disgust that is often called visceral (it "makes one sick" or "makes one vomit") for everything that is facile'.[13] While this is a problem in itself – how pure can 'pure taste' be if it is constituted only by negation? – perhaps the most important and debilitating consequence of taste is the confinement of aesthetic forms which deviate from the dominant taste to the margins of theoretical interest. This does not mean that no aesthetic judgements or exclusions are possible on the grounds of taste, nor that judgements or exclusions are entirely without justification, nor indeed that taste must always operate as a covert form of socio-economic oppression. What it does mean, however, is that one has to accept fundamentally, as a political *a priori*, that notions of taste have unavoidable consequences for the way we view and write about cinema. That is, our canons and theories are ultimately transitory and arbitrary in respect to the dominant economy of taste. In contrast, film theory has historically envisioned itself as an end in itself, setting itself up as the touchstone of cinematic taste. It is in this sense that we should be prepared to interrogate and push back the frontiers of those theories and canons themselves in order to understand exactly to what extent they serve to delimit rather than expand our knowledge of cinema. And it is in this sense that exploitation assumes its true historical and theoretical significance, for it provides a parallax view through which the domains of history and theory can be rethought.

The interdependence of the technological history/development of cinema and forms of cinematic exploitation has been asserted, denied and generally commented upon by film theorists and historians. Yet film theory has tended to rapidly pass over this relationship, favouring instead analysis of plot, narrative and character, and so avoiding the issues that such a recognition of interdependence might raise. The problems are indeed extremely complex, and the implications of recognising them prove to be far-reaching for the ways in which we understand and write about both exploitation film and cinema in general. Moreover, a consideration of the technological and economic history of the cinema, and of its immediate precursors, inevitably touches on the status and function of cinema as a semiotic/ideological/pleasure practice, which in turn opens up a host of further problems: what is the aesthetic and economic relationship between exploitation and non-exploitation film?; who or what is being exploited and by what process is this effected?; and, more fundamentally, is it ultimately possible and/or useful to designate a body of films as exploitation and if so, then what purpose does it serve? In the face of this, the safest option, and the one that has been adopted by Film Studies, is to avoid the problem altogether, or, if it cannot be avoided, to regard the pre-history and origins of cinematic technologies and commercial structures as irrevocably separate and/or incommensurable with the present situation. In this way no existing notions about the cinematic fact or institution need be upset and writers need not venture too far from well-trodden paths. However, this view simply ignores, first, that *all* forms of cinema exist within the social process of cinema as a whole, and, second, that the history of exploitation cannot be isolated from the aesthetic and economic history of cinema in general.

In the optical inventions of the late nineteenth century – cameras, magic lanterns, zoetropes, kinetographs, kinetoscopes and the early precursors to cinema – we can see a powerful manifestation of both the formal and aesthetic development of exploitation and, perhaps more crucially, the socio-economic relationship established between the film and its audience which would later come to define exploitation cinema. Moreover, in Eadweard Muybridge's photographic motion studies, the prototypical precursors to cinematic technology, we can begin to recognise how the desire to see and know more of the possibilities and limits of the human body underlies the very invention of cinema itself. By the same token, advances in early film technologies and the evolution of formal techniques were often directly linked to and/or dependent (either economically or formally) on the desire to show in ever more detail the mechanics of the human form to a paying public. In this respect, Linda Williams argues that 'the very invention of cinema develops, to a certain extent, from the desire to place the clocked and measured bodies produced by the first machines into narratives that naturalise their movements'.[14] Thus, both the economic and aesthetic development of the institution of cinema went hand in hand with developing pleasures of the new medium. So, if Muybridge's first audiences came simply to see and learn the scientific 'truths' of bodily motion, they stayed and/or returned to see more precisely because this newly acquired knowledge was also infused with an unsuspected visual pleasure – a pleasure with enormous commercial potential. In other words, the appeal of seeing the first humans walking across a gridded space and later performing all kinds of contortions and tasks was thus never purely scientific in origin. Indeed, in Muybridge's longer and more sustained examples of naked bodies, Williams claims that 'we begin to see an illustration of Foucault's point that the power exerted over bodies *in* technology is rendered pleasurable *through* technology'.[15] Similarly, at the moment of cinematic origin, social, cultural, technological and economic discourses intersect to channel the scientific discovery of bodily motion/spectacle into new forms of pleasure and corresponding new commercial possibilities. What is at stake here is that the socio-technological institution of cinema and exploitation film are not independent inventions, with the latter simply being grafted onto the pre-existing apparatus of the former; their specific historical and social construction began simultaneously with the invention of cinema itself. To cite Williams again:

> If Muybridge's prototypical cinema became rather quickly ... a photographic girlie show that belied its more serious pretensions, it is not because men are more naturally voyeurs and fetishists and that these perverse pleasures overwhelmed science. Rather, science and perversion interpenetrated in the construction of cinematic discourse.[16]

With the invention of cinema, in other words, fetishism and voyeurism – the desire to see and know more – gained new importance and, to some extent, became normalised through their genealogical link to Muybridge's scientific discourse. Moreover, it is no accident that the fusion of the voyeuristic drive and the scopophilic possibilities of the celluloid image became instantaneously bound up with the commercial–economic agenda of the new medium. Right from those earliest days audiences were willing to pay for the privilege of 'seeing human bodies in motion in the better way afforded by cinema' and came to expect that it would 'include these perverse pleasures as a matter of course'.[17] In this sense, then, Muybridge's pre-historic cinema established the configuration of aesthetic, psychic and economic discourses necessary for cinema to exist in the socio-cultural formation in its present state; that is, in a post-industrial media economy.

It is precisely the intersection of economic, aesthetic and psychic discourses, configured as they were in the origins of cinema, that is often mobilised in order to define exploitation film as a cinematic idiom distinct from that of mainstream/ dominant cinema. In general terms, the label of exploitation has been applied to a form of cinema that attempts to 'grab an audience by offering something unavailable elsewhere – films that pander to our baser instincts, pique our curiosity, salaciously sell us the seamier side of life, but do so knowingly and for one basic reason – to make money'.[18] The discourses invoked here in order to separate exploitation cinema from the default category of cinema are identical to the aesthetic, socio-psychic and economic discourses which catalysed both the technological invention of cinema and its inception into the socio-cultural process. More specifically, the desire to see and to know more about the capabilities, limits and forms of the human body and its relationship to the environment not only provides the audience with a set of visual and psychic pleasures 'unavailable elsewhere', but also provides the film-maker/institution with a basic commodity that can be exploited/marketed for maximum economic return.

In this respect, exploitation cinema approaches Tom Gunning's definition of 'The cinema of attractions'. In an invigorating discussion of the genealogy of cinematic narration, Gunning reminds us that early cinema reflected a marked absence of preoccupations with creating a self-sufficient narrative diegesis on the screen. In fact, he suggests that in the prototypical years of cinema, it was cinema itself that was the attraction, not the fictions it projected. Moreover, the cinema of attractions directly solicited spectator attention by

> inciting visual curiosity, and supplying pleasure through an exciting spectacle ... Theatrical display dominates over narrative absorption, emphasising the direct simulation of shock or surprise at the expense of unfolding a story or creating a diegetic universe ... Making use of both fictional and non-fictional attractions, its energy moves outward towards an acknowledged spectator rather than inward toward the character-based situations essential to classical narrative.[19]

Here the notion of exploitation coalesces around the nodal point of exhibition/consumption. The interrelation between the audience and the cinematic institutions can be seen as a function of the fact that films, or rather viewings of films, are commodities of a specific kind. In the same way that Muybridge's motion studies were made in the guise of scientific discovery but were almost instantaneously co-opted by commercial agencies, so exploitation cinema is a convenient category in which aesthetic and formal considerations are organised with capital investment/assets so as to ensure that their economic potential will be utilised to maximum commercial effect. Given this, the *exploitation* of exploitation cinema approaches Stephen Neale's definition of genre – genre not in the iconographic or narrative senses, but rather in terms of the economic functioning of genre. For genres clearly exist within the context of a set of economic relations and practices, a point often stressed by pointing out that they are the *forms* of the *products* of capital-intensive cinema: 'Films are, and have been from the earliest days of Hollywood, produced and marketed as Westerns and Comedies and so on ... The standardisation of product obliged by the economic necessities of large scale industrial production led to studios concentrating on particular genres ... for that purpose.'[20] However, economic factors do not lead inexorably to genre. The familiar argument that there is an inevitable tendency towards genre in the conditions of economic exchange under capitalism may be true at a general level insofar as the pressures for profitability that underlie capital-intensive film-making demand a framework of (financial) guarantees, it can nevertheless be misleading on the level of the individual film. For capitalist relations can ultimately account neither for the existence of specific genres, nor for the formal and aesthetic conventions that constitute them. This is not to sever generic questions from economic ones. On the contrary, as Neale notes, if understood as a framework for production and as a form of organisation of cinema's product, genre 'clearly has a relationship to economic factors' and is clearly, at least in part, 'determined by them'.[21] And it seems to me that the fundamental axioms of that relationship are to be found, on the one hand, in the functioning of genre in relation to the exigency for profit, and, on the other hand, in relation to the tensions generated in the gap between cinema's dual status as art and commerce. Neale helps clarify this vexing situation. He argues that

> When linked to the fact of economic pressures toward maximisation of capital assets, and to the concomitant forms of production organisation these pressures give rise to, the economic importance of genre becomes evident: genres serve as basic and 'convenient' units for the calculation of investment and profit, and as basic and 'convenient' categories in which to organise capital assets so as to ensure that their capacity will be utilised to the maximum. Economic factors can therefore be seen to exert a pressure which results, not perhaps in the creation of genres as such, but rather in their perpetuation as the basic form that the industry's products take.[22]

While strictly speaking economics cannot define exploitation film as a genre, it nevertheless can account for the ways in which it tends to occupy much of the same ground as genre film, because films are planned and constructed according to an economic imperative. From this point of view, the economic function of genre is crucial to our understanding of exploitation cinema, for it provides not only 'maximum regularity and economy in the utilisation of plant and personnel', but also 'the minimum degree of difference necessary for each individual product'.[23]

Exploitation film is thus brought into focus as a blatantly commercial product, sold on the basis of its apparent revelatory qualities, and designed to ensure maximum possible return from the minimum investment and resources. To that extent the exploitation film itself is defined as a *proactive* commodity in the sense that it *exploits* its audience for economic purposes. By implication, this suggests that the audience is *passive*. But now we confront the political and theoretical difficulty of the whole exploitation debate, where the binarist paradigm of active/passive fails to comprehend its inherent entropy. For simply positing a binary configuration of exploiter/exploited does not account for the possibility that the discourse of exploitation may in fact straddle the material duality of production/consumption. In other words, it discounts the way in which specific cultural determinants may at times not only outweigh the significance of economics, but thoroughly shift the grounds on which the exploitation constitutes itself (and is constituted). And perhaps most importantly any binary description of exploitation not only belies its compound production, its mutual and contradictory inscription by text and audience, but also ignores the pleasures imbricated in the discourses of exploitation as well. As such, it becomes necessary to discuss the intersection between economic factors and pleasure, between product and audience, and to propose a much more complicated relation between the two than simply a polarised play between active and passive.

Cinema's commodity, its consumable product, is film, and more often than not narrative film. However, cinema's commodity is peculiar inasmuch as it is not, strictly speaking, the film itself that is for sale. That is, what the consumer's money buys is not the film as such but the privilege to view it. Moreover, this privilege is not the privilege that attends owning a product in the empirical sense, but the privileged access to a *process*. John Ellis outlines this unique trading relationship as follows:

> To say that cinema produces films is painfully inadequate: films as strips of celluloid in cans are without great value, certainly not meriting the amount expended on their production ... Films, then, are themselves processes rather than products: capital is turned over by the industry through people paying to see a film, not to buy a copy of it ... These processes ... effect a perpetual placing of the subject in relation to desire – a continual process that we are pleased to call pleasurable.[24]

The main problem for the industry, stemming from this situation, is that it needs, as far as possible, to guarantee the meanings and pleasures of its product in order to solicit and sustain an audience large enough to produce surplus revenue to satisfy its investors. To do so, the industry is compelled to institutionalise a set of textual and social expectations which it will be able, within the parameters of its economic and ideological remit, consistently to fulfil and which can be utilised in various ways in order to regulate desire and control demand across a series of textual instances. This operates on a number of levels ranging from the star system to generic structures and narrative systems. However, exploitation cinema guarantees meaning and pleasure *and* maintains audiences capable of returning a profit predominantly through its marketing and promotional strategies, which institutionalise coherence and foreclose meaning by guaranteeing the fulfilment of institutionalised expectations prior to watching the film. Exploitation can therefore be defined as a film practice 'in which the elements of plot and acting are subordinate to elements that can be promoted'.[25] Herschell Gordon Lewis, a director and producer of many exploitation films, elaborates on this idea. He states, 'That's exploitation – elements the promoter can grab on to and shake in the face of theatre owners to get them to play the picture and in the face of the public to get them to see it.'[26] Exploitation becomes defined, not in terms of the film itself, but by the means in which it is sold to its potential audience. It is not so much a systematic discourse, as generic definitions necessarily imply, but rather a discourse of systemisation.

At this point the various discourses mobilised to constitute exploitation cinema, and the various problems and contradictions raised by those discourses, can be brought together. All exploitation is simultaneously an active *and* passive process: as the object of exploitation it is passive – a commercially driven product in which capital assets are configured in such a way as to ensure maximum economic profit; as the subject effecting the exploitation the film is active – a self-conscious commodity which caters for the desires of its paying audience in order to fulfil its economic project.

However, just as exploitation defies generic definitions, it is insufficient to argue that exploitation cinema is merely designated by a subordination of the fictional process to elements that can be sold in the marketplace. This simply ignores the fact that all films exist within the context of economic relations and practices, and that all films, to a greater or lesser extent, organise capital assets so that their potential capacity will be utilised to the maximum. For this reason Lewis regards *Jurassic Park* 'as the ultimate exploitation picture'.[27] Moreover, the process of selling and financing a film on the basis of a concept or series of key scenes is by no means exclusive to exploitation, but in fact dominates contemporary film production in Hollywood and throughout the world. The economic facts of cinematic life dictate that an industrially viable cinema requires large amounts of capital to be invested in a project before it goes into production. Investors channel money not into a finished movie, but into a concept, an idea, a package, which will be marketed in such a way so as to best ensure a profit. Indeed, the commercial drama surrounding a movie's promotion can say as much today as the fictional drama of the film itself. Hollywood productions now seem to aspire to be successfully understood and enjoyed without even being seen. The promotional drama itself provides a cultural text that invariably exceeds and outlives the movie it prefigures. Likewise, many of the pleasures associated with contemporary cinema lie in the gestalt image of a film in the public image of its promotion. The important point is, however, that this was also the attraction of exploitation: the foreknowledge of the spectacle.

Given that this is the case, consideration of exploitation must involve two distinct, but nevertheless overlapping moments. First, a historical moment. Exploitation cinema represents a specific period in cinematic history in which the specific configuration of socio-economic discourses and censorship legislation provided an environment that enabled film-makers and studios to exploit this relationship for economic purposes. The establishment of the Hays Office in 1921 and its subsequent consolidation in the MPPDA code of conduct (together with a corresponding tightening of censorship laws throughout Western Europe) thwarted the pleasures and desires established in the moment of cinema's invention, which were bound up in exhibiting the limits, capabilities and form of the human body. Thus, it was the interpenetration of cinematic and censorship discourses that (inevitably) (re)created the desire for illicit and revelatory images. The introduction of censorship legislation actively created the illicit subjects, and by extension the salacious material for the film to exploit. This approach emphasises the need to understand the dynamics of exploitation cinema within its own cultural formation and as part of a specific historical conjuncture. And it is this approach that continues to dominate the study of exploitation.

However, while this procedure provides an important redress to dominant histories of cinema, it runs the risk of being a dead end, or at least an end in itself. By bracketing the cinematic regimes defined as exploitation with history, the specificity of exploitation, that is the terms on which it functions and has been transposed into the present, becomes lost from sight. My question then is: what model of analysis is able to account for the differences *as well as* the connections between exploitation's historical manifestations and the present situation? For the issue of exploitation is as much a question of address as a matter of history or even economics. This leads us to the second moment: the present.

Exploitation – the embodiment of tastelessness – is now itself, paradoxically, part of dominant taste, and its processes and discourses have become integral even to cinema's most official and mainstream manifestations. This suggests that if the concept of exploitation survives today, it does so neither as a paracinema, a beyond, an outside to cinema, nor as 'cultural detritus' or the 'cinematic dregs' that Sconce describes. Nor is it an intrinsically oppositional discourse, a 'bad film' counter-aesthetic capable of filling the void vacated by the historical avant-gardes. On the contrary, the significance of exploitation cinema now lies precisely in its proximity to the present capital-intensive patterns of film production. That is, if the concept of the exploitation film can be translated into the present at all, it is as a framework for discussing the production and marketing strategies of the most mainstream manifestation of cinema – Hollywood. The dangers of not conducting both operations at the same time are all too familiar. Starting from a position of challenging the histories which dominate conceptions of cinema, it becomes all too tempting to privilege the former moment at the expense of the latter and construct a new imaginary unity. This often leads to the establishment of an anti-canon of cult cinema which is celebrated for its apparent opposition to the mainstream. What is missing from this overtly retroactive (but otherwise unobjectionable) practice is precisely exploitation's relevance to the present. Only by investigating both moments simultaneously, in a dialectical movement, can notions of exploitation be deployed against the universalising economy of taste in Film Studies, to expel the Euro-American bourgeois conceptions of cinema from the centre of film history and critical theory. For it is in the marriage of past and present, of history and theory, that the study of exploitation cinema can avoid the self-enclosed reductionism of much current work on trash and cult movies and achieve that elusive goal of being able to teach us something about our present situation as well as providing a corrective to the myopia of history.

Of course, these few notes provide only an overly schematic and somewhat reductive account of the complexity of the historical and socio-economic discourses at play in the idea of exploitation cinema. However, such a schematic account at least allows for a clear understanding of why exploitation has proved such a difficult discourse to accommodate within the established networks of film theory and historiography which, by recourse to the principles of taste and its own ensconced canons of excellence, relegates it to the fringes of (para?)academia. Nevertheless, a number of conclusions follow from this primary reconnaissance of the terrain. First, the definition of exploitation cinema needs to be rethought vis-a-vis orthodox film history and theory. While exploitation, as a general socio-cultural phenomenon, is not reducible to exploitation as a (critically constructed) genre of discourse and textuality, equally exploitation film practices, and the discourses that comprise it, are not simply reducible to a socio-cultural process. And to the extent that exploitation is constituted historically, it is founded not only in the psychic and aesthetic origins of cinema but also in the socio-economic discursive configuration that inaugurated its inception into the socio-cultural formation. The issue, then, becomes the extent to which histories of the cinema are also histories of exploitation, how far it is possible to disintricate the two sets of structures associated with them at particular moments in history. The schema according to which exploitation cinema is distinguished from the institution and history of cinema should be abandoned, and attention turned to the historio-graphic, aesthetic and economic discursive structures through which all cinema operates. All these areas of practice contribute fundamentally to the recognition that *all* cinema is, to a greater or lesser extent, exploitation cinema. Moreover, a recognition of the fact that a whole set of different discourses are at play in the all-encompassing phrase of 'the institution of cinema' is an essential first step in reconstituting histories of the cinema, and thus to unblock a number of the contradictions dogging the work of film critics.

I want to end by reiterating my own political–intellectual agenda, which is not to appropriate exploitation cinema for popular culture, nor to celebrate 'bad film' for its own sake, but to place the problems and issues it raises for film theory and historiography squarely in the field of contemporary film practices. This means that one does not simply (re)produce a context in which the relative aesthetic and cultural merits of historical exploitation are measured in terms of the present economy of taste. Exploitation provides an important aesthetic and political prism through which the entire domain of cinematic theory can be rethought in the context of taste. In negotiating this increasingly urgent manoeuvre, film theory may confront itself precisely where it has convinced itself it should not exist: establishing conceptual alliances no longer reducible to the stultifying laws of taste.

Notes

1. Pierre Bourdieu, *Distinction: A Social Critique of the Judgement of Taste* (London: Routledge, 1986), p. 47.
2. For a discussion of cinephilia, see Paul Willemen, 'Through the glass darkly: cinephilia reconsidered', *Looks and Frictions* (London: BFI, 1994).
3. Jeffrey Sconce, 'Trashing the academy: taste, excess and an emerging politics of cinematic style', *Screen* 36, 4 (Winter, 1995), p. 372. See also Steve Chibnall, this volume.
4. Ibid.
5. Bourdieu, *Distinction*, p. 6.
6. Ibid., p. 7.
7. Ibid., p. 57.
8. Ibid., p. 56.

9. Ibid.
10. V. Vale and Andrea Juno (eds), *Re/Search #10, Incredibly Strange Films* (San Francisco: Re/Search, 1986), p. 4.
11. Bourdieu, *Distinction*, p. 57.
12. Ibid., p. 486.
13. Ibid.
14. Linda Williams, *Hard Core* (London: Pandora, 1990), p. 36.
15. Ibid., p. 39.
16. Ibid., p. 45.
17. Ibid., p. 46.
18. Jonathan Ross, *The Incredibly Strange Film Book: An Alternative History of Cinema* (New York: Simon and Schuster, 1995), p. 63.
19. Tom Gunning, 'The cinema of attractions', *Wide Angle* 8, 3/4 (Fall, 1986).
20. Tom Ryall, 'Teaching through genre', *Screen Education* 17, p. 27.
21. Stephen Neale, *Genre* (London: BFI, 1980), p. 52.
22. Ibid.
23. Ibid., p. 53.
24. John Ellis, 'The institution of cinema', *Edinburgh '77 Magazine* (1977), p. 37.
25. Herschell Gordon Lewis, in John McCarty (ed.), *The Sleaze Merchants: Adventures in Exploitation Film Making* (New York: St Martin's Press, 1995), p. 38.
26. Ibid., p. 39.
27. David Friedman in McCarty, *The Sleaze Merchants*, p. 38.

5

Double Exposures: Observations on *The Flesh and Blood Show*

Steve Chibnall

> He conceals his shame with such cultural mechanisms as pop, camp, and trivia, but ... [his] intellectual guilt compels him to deny serious purpose and individual artistry to the mass spectacles he has been educated to despise.
>
> Andrew Sarris on the academic film critic[1]

Exploitation films were once cinema's most humble and vilified creations. Generations of critics condemned them as the monstrous creatures of unscrupulous directorial Frankensteins pieced together like reconstituted corpses from the remains of more noble cinematic lives, and re-animated for undemanding viewers to the financial aggrandisement of their makers. Easily dismissed as meretricious rather than meritorious, they were seen to 'pander' to cinema-goers hungry for emotional sensation rather than cerebral stimulation. As texts, their meanings were apparently as transparent as their narratives were formulaic, and any value that might accrue to them must be an accident of their construction, context or unpredictable adoption by cultish audiences. Academically, these disreputable films were of interest primarily for their alleged deleterious effects on viewers (promoting either violence or a dominant ideology), or for the ways in which they might exhibit symptoms of cultural malaise and social pathology. Challenges to this critical orthodoxy began in the early 1960s with auteurism, but this represented a recuperation of popular commercial cinema rather than the wilder shores of exploitation. The New York avant-garde had actively promoted a 'trash aesthetic' and the camp appeal of excessiveness in texts had long been appreciated by critics,[2] but by the end of the

1970s there had been few attempts to spotlight exploitation films for critical consideration. That changed in the early 1980s with a wave of American publications dedicated to 'bad' and 'cult' films. This new discourse was the illicit progeny of a tryst between disreputable films and respectable college students in the back rows of the Midnight Movie. Its authors bridged the gap between the academy and the post-war generation of extramural cinephiles and trash aesthetes.

The initial pioneers in the uncharted realms of American bad taste were the culturally conservative Medveds.[3] Their searches for the worst movies ever made combined camp appreciation with a cynical dismissal that alienated cinephiles who wanted to celebrate low-budget exploitation cinema for the challenge it posed to dominant judgements of taste and aesthetics. This more serious strain of appreciation can be found in work ranging from the raw enthusiasm of Michael Weldon for weird and bizarre 'psychotronic' films, through John McCarty's valorisations of 'splatter movies' and poverty-row auteurs, to Danny Peary's canonising of emergent 'cult' movies.[4] The criteria of value employed by these authors are not always explicit or consistent, but strangeness and excess are well to the fore and there is a glorification of banality, especially when combined with surprising cinematic innovation (despite or, perhaps, because of the lowness of budgets).

Politically, the new psychotronic criticism ran counter to dominant streams of political correctness in the academy. Although aware of feminism and the politics of difference, the new criticism shows no desire to 'do the right thing', but rather to ironically elevate texts that often exhibit a naive disregard for sexism, misogyny, racism and other pre-enlightenment sins. Drawing on developing feelings of disempowerment and marginality among straight white males, the psychotronic sensibility was a reassertion of the right to look, to make anything the object of the knowing, sardonic, ironising and frankly excited gaze.[5] Thus, what unites most psychotronic aficionados is the rejection of censorship for adult viewers and the insistent need, so prevalent among the generation of 'baby-boomers', to expose what was previously hidden (sleaze).[6] The exposure itself becomes an act of empowerment enhanced by reactions of shock and disbelief in others. The satisfactions it supplies offer relief from the chronic *ennui* engendered by media overload. The result has been the generation of new fields of fandom served by a plethora of amateur and professional fanzines with assiduous researchers unearthing esoteric knowledge about forgotten films, fresh sources of alternative cultural capital for autodidacts.[7]

The reasons for the emergence of serious interest in disreputable films at a particular moment in the USA are a combination of opportunity and predisposition. Five points are relevant.

First, the system of film exhibition in America during the 1970s offered opportunities to see low-budget and independent movies which were unavailable in the UK. Drive-ins and struggling downtown movie theatres screened exploitation sleaze which could be appropriated for late-night showings by more respectable cinemas with a strong student clientele. 'Midnight Movies' also played incessantly on American network and cable television, attracting audiences beyond those originally targeted by their producers and leading to alternative modes of appreciation. Theatrical exhibition and broadcasting, therefore, created a dislocation of the taken-for-granted relationship between exploitation films and their audiences which became possible in the UK only with the arrival of video. In Britain, television stations closed down at midnight and late-night cinema screenings were largely confined to major metropolitan centres and the showing of 'arthouse' films.

Second, the midnight movie phenomenon meshed with postmodern intellectual trends towards cultural relativism and the celebration of difference to elevate some exploitation films into an alternative canon of 'cult' films. The notion of 'cult' effectively collapses the categories of 'art' and 'exploitation', eliding issues of both politics and aesthetics. What might previously have been distinguished according to the motivations of their makers were now rendered largely equivalent by the enthusiastic and loyal responses of audiences possessing different types of cultural capital. Cinematic 'gold', it seemed, might be found in the most unlikely places and the search was on to discover more.

Third, the scrambling of categoric distinctions evidenced in the identification of cult movies was complemented in Hollywood by textual practices which ironically reversed the economic and artistic relationships between exploitation film and mainstream cinema. 'Movie brat' film-makers such as Steven Spielberg and George Lucas began to take the low-budget adventure movies of their childhoods and recreate them as big budget, hyper-real spectaculars. Instead of exploitation film being parasitic on the narratives and conventions of mainstream cinema, the Hollywood blockbuster became increasingly dependent for inspiration on the pulp fictions of the cinematic past. Whereas once they had been banished to the catacombs, old exploitation films now all became candidates for resurrection, awaiting an enterprising sponsor.

Fourth, the cultural entrepreneurship of the new generation of cinéaste directors resulted not only in the commercial resuscitation of comatose exploitation product, but also in the critical recuperation of maverick texts by film-makers with authorial credentials. Familiar examples include Martin Scorsese's championing of Michael Powell's much-maligned *Peeping Tom* (1960) and John Waters' hailing of Russ Meyer's *Faster, Pussycat, Kill Kill!* (1966) as the greatest movie of all time.[8]

Fifth, it was impossible for the academy to be left untouched by this destabilising of taste and the effects were quickly apparent in the fracturing of hegemonic paradigms within film studies, particularly those approaches which Janet Staiger identifies as romantic auteurism and ideological criticism.[9] The shock waves would slowly cross the Atlantic to Britain, combining with feminist film theory's assault on ideas of universality of meaning and interpretation to severely damage the foundations of that hybrid of Marxism and psychoanalysis known as '*Screen* theory'.[10] A space was cleared for heretical reading practices less dismissive of popular pleasure and desire, and the extension of the academic frame of reference to include what Jeffrey Sconce terms 'paracinema' – the weird, the trashy and the psychotronic.[11] Paracinema has provided opportunities for (predominantly) young straight white male academics to reclaim marginalised areas of cinema's history and to resist the dominant paradigms of film theory which have tended to problematise and pathologise male heterosexual pleasure in the text.

The early 1980s were a watershed in the discourse around exploitation and cult films not just because of the growth of fanzines/magazines and major critical studies but because of profound changes in the modes of film consumption. Exploitation films (particularly those of the 1970s) were among the earliest movies available in the new format of home video cassette, giving them a second life and a prominence they had rarely enjoyed in the cinema. Consequently, the distinction between timeless classics and ephemeral pulp began to dissolve as they shared the same rental shelves. Nowhere was this more true than in Britain where video offered an outlet for films denied any substantial screen time by the restrictive practices of cinema distributors and exhibitors and television schedulers. Britain adopted the video revolution faster and more enthusiastically than any other country,[12] but in America, too, video would have profound implications for the appreciation of disreputable films and their progress to cult status.

In the 1970s, the Midnight Movie movement had provided the opportunity for communal celebrations of difference at late-night screenings, but video transformed films from collective experiences to privatised commodities which may be used (like any others) in the process of individual identity formation and communication. At the same time as video commodification was shifting film consumption from the public to the private sphere, the new psychotronic criticism was moving knowledge and awareness of cult and disreputable cinema out of its narrow subcultural confines and into more publicly-accessible domains. The immediate effect of this was to increase the power of the critic at the expense of the film exhibitor. Henceforth, cult movies would be more often born in the pages of zines than at midnight screenings, and the attribution of cult status to exploitation film would be the result of subjective discursive practices rather than observable audience response.

My contention, then, is that the romantic model of cult movie creation by gregarious misfits at midnight box offices is becoming increasingly outmoded. We are already witnessing concerted marketing attempts to confer cult status on texts even before they reach our cinema and television screens,[13] and publications for a popular market that apply the cult label to collections of films while paying no more than lip service to the idea of special audience response. For example, Welch Everman's criteria of inclusion in his *Cult Horror Films* rely almost exclusively on aspects of their textuality once the basic criteria of being made 'strictly for the horror audience' has been met. Everman effortlessly consecrates exploitation films simply by writing (often breathtakingly banal) reviews of them for fellow horror fans. His selection criteria are too idiosyncratic to identify the shared textual elements of exploitation films which might mark them out for special attention, but his connection to the College of Arts and Humanities at the University of Maine at least indicates the degree to which fan sensibilities and preoccupations are taking root in the academy.[14]

During the 1980s and 1990s there has been not only a continuing expansion of Film Studies in Britain and the US but also a developing interpenetration between academic (cinéaste) film culture and extramural fan (cinephile) culture. This has been most clearly evident in the mutual interest in the popular genres of science fiction and horror. Cinéastes and cinephiles still speak in different tongues but they increasingly talk about the same movies. If I am correct, academic criteria of judgement and discursive concerns will become increasingly influential in the recuperating and cultish appropriation of disreputable films.

To illustrate the potential intellectual interest contained within unheralded exploitation pictures I will offer the case study of a British genre film from the early 1970s, *The Flesh and Blood Show* (1972). An early British example of a subgenre of the horror film that would later be called 'stalk and slash',[15] it features a mysterious killer who picks off members of an isolated group of young people in a gory and erotic extension of the classic murder mystery. Although the conventions of 'stalk and slash' had already been introduced by Alfred Hitchcock and Mario Bava, *The Flesh and Blood Show* was made six years before *Halloween* (1978) began the main cycle of American 'slasher' movies. The film was self-financed by its producer and director, Peter Walker, a one-time actor and comedian who had begun his movie-making career by photographing and distributing 8mm 'glamour' films in the soft-core *Heritage* range. Walker had attracted a little favourable critical attention with his fifth film, a wryly comic and disturbingly amoral permissive drama *Cool It Carol* (1970), and was starting to make the transition to what he would call 'terror pictures' – some of the most perverse and disturbing of all British horror films.[16]

The Flesh and Blood Show was Walker's eighth film in five years and, although vigorously promoted in the US by the notorious sexploitation entrepreneur, David Friedman, it has remained obscure, even to most horror film devotees. Its current reputation among horror fans is as a rather slow and predictable whodunit with too little blood-letting to satisfy the dedicated gore-hound.[17] In spite of recent festival screenings at Hampstead, in London, and Leicester,[18] and its distinctive use of 3-D technology, *The Flesh and Blood Show* has yet to achieve the minor cult status enjoyed by Walker's *House of Whipcord* (1974) and *Frightmare* (1974). The strongest indicator of impending celebrity is the high value on the collectors' market of the rare UK Vampix video release of the film (available only in the early 1980s).

Although *The Flesh and Blood Show* achieved only limited success with its original viewers and has attracted few plaudits from critics[19] and modern audiences, its screenplay by Alfred Shaughnessy is one of the most complex and interesting of any British exploitation film. There are many features of its textuality which satisfy the criteria of cultishness developed in the academic literature. Beneath its meretricious surfaces lies a subtextual life which is rich enough in latent meanings, allusions and autobiographical elements to suggest that there is an implied audience which has yet to discover its mysteries.

The Flesh and Blood Show went into production in the winter of 1971–72 in its director's home town, Brighton, where a disused theatre at the end of the West Pier was the principal location. The ensemble cast featured Ray Brooks – *The Knack* (1965), *Cathy Come Home* (1966) – and two actresses, Jenny Hanley and Luan Peters, already known for their work in Hammer horror films. However, it is the presence in the cast of Robin Askwith, that icon of 1970s masculinity, which is most likely to enhance the film's cult credentials among modern British audiences.

The plot of *The Flesh and Blood Show* mirrors the conditions of the film's production. A disparate collection of young actors, brought together by an unseen producer, assemble in an icy old theatre to rehearse an entertainment called 'The Flesh and Blood Show'. We see them picked off by a mysterious assassin, who turns out to be a distinguished actor (long thought to be dead) who has taken on the persona of Othello, a part he played 25 years before. In exploitation terms, this provides a framework for creepy suspense, gruesome death and titillating flashes of nudity from the attractive female cast. But it is the ways in which the film transcends the diegetic boundaries of exploitation cinema that command attention and establish its principal claims to cult status. As J.P. Telotte argues in *The Cult Film Experience:* 'What the film cultist embraces is a form that, in its very difference, transgresses, violates our sense of the reasonable. It crosses the boundaries of time, custom, form, and – many might add – good taste.'[20]

In his own seminal analysis of cult movies, Umberto Eco introduces the notion of a fractured bricolage of styles, ideas and fragments from other texts which give the cult film a ramshackle quality, allowing it to become 'unhinged' from its generic structures. He argues that it should 'display not one central idea but many. It should not reveal a coherent philosophy of composition. It must live on, and because of, its glorious ricketiness. However, it must have some quality.'[21] *The Flesh and Blood Show* conforms ideally to Eco's model. It mixes Agatha Christie's *Ten Little Niggers* (1939) with a Warner Brothers backstage musical, adding lashings of French Grand Guignol melodrama and Shakespearian references and tossing in some gratuitous 3-D effects. The themes and sensibilities of the Italian *giallo* are given the most quintessential of English settings in a narrative that struggles against submersion in its powerful subtexts. This film is certainly 'unhinged', not least in its deliberate confusion of high and low cultural referencing. In a cult movie like *Casablanca* (1942), Eco suggests we see not 'real' life 'but life as stereotypically portrayed in previous films'.[22] This mediated world is ever present in Walker's pictures, which frequently replay cinematic memories, culminating in *The House of the Long Shadows* (1983), a full-blown pastiche of the old dark house school of Gothic melodrama. In *The Flesh and Blood Show* the historical quotations are more eclectic, ranging from William Castle's camp special effects gimmicks, through *Stage Fright* (1950) to *The Phantom of the Opera* (1925, 1943). In an important sense, however the whole film can be seen as a homage to George Cukor's Oscar-winning *A Double Life* (1947) in which Ronald Colman stars as a stage actor who succumbs to the same murderous obsessions as his character, Othello.[23] Eco refers to the effect of texts whose fragments constantly echo other films as a 'sense of déjà vu'; and in one bizarrely self-referential moment in *The Flesh and Blood Show*, Ray Brooks actually takes the time to explain the phenomenon of déjà vu to Jenny Hanley: 'We jump for a split second into a subconscious where there is no time. It's an illusion of repetition. We see the past, present and future all at once because our four-dimensional view of it doesn't fix it in time.' Such incongruous discourse in a slasher movie is another example of this film's unhinged 'personality', but also relates directly to its thematic structure.

The juxtaposing of present and past is one of the dualities around which Alfred Shaughnessy's screenplay is organised. Shaughnessy, best known for his work on the successful television series *Upstairs, Downstairs* (1970–75), was already an experienced scriptwriter and director with a background – Eton and Sandhurst – that challenges our easy assumptions about exploitation film writers. Hammer studios had recently produced his script for the psychological thriller, *Crescendo* (1969), but his first horror film had been as director and script editor of the Lewtonesque *Cat Girl* (1957). Themes evident in these earlier films – jealousy, repressed passions, the malign legacy of the past and dual identity – would reappear in *The Flesh and Blood Show*, but only here are they accompanied by such an extraordinary degree of self-reflexivity.

The Flesh and Blood Show lays bare the mechanics of exploitation presentations. The title itself draws attention to its theatricality and the audience's desire for visceral sensation or, as the American publicity put it, 'carnage and carnality'. The showing of flesh and blood was the key constituent of

British exploitation cinema in its most highly developed form between 1969 and 1979. Such a display was a necessary compensation for the poverty of budgets in this period as American capital was recalled home. Nudity and gore cheaply provided that frisson of excitement craved by (male) viewers and, because of the challenge this posed to censorship restrictions, could be regarded as culturally transgressive, and even politically progressive, by spectators who identified with ideas and lifestyles of the counter-culture. *The Flesh and Blood Show* associates this interest in explicit theatrical displays with an ascendent youth culture (the company of young actors), while implying that the same tastes in their parents' generation had been suppressed by strict morality and censorship. Walker's picture shows the flesh and blood consequences of that moment when the young theatre of permissiveness meets a much older theatre of cruelty, whose resentful representative is driven to sadistic violence by repressed desire and failing hegemonic power.

Walker and Shaughnessy were not the first exploitation film-makers to offer a deconstruction of their own enterprise.[24] The classic precursor is, of course, Michael Powell's incomparable *Peeping Tom* whose similar stalk and slash narrative implicates the audience in a powerful critique of voyeurism in cinema. But, whereas *Peeping Tom* emphasises the role of the viewer in the exploitation spectacle (the looking), *The Flesh and Blood Show* concentrates on the contribution of the actor (the showing). To make a display of oneself in an exploitation epic like this one, it suggests, is to prostitute one's art, and to invite the righteous wrath of the great knights of the stage like the film's avenging assassin Sir Arnold Gates. Sir Arnold castigates the youth of his profession: 'They're all the same, young actors – filthy and degenerate lechers – all of them. And the females, flaunting their bodies, offering their thighs and their breasts. Scum! Excrement!'

In both Sir Arnold's imagination and the film's scenarios, acting and promiscuity are closely connected. Actors are necessarily faithless and their commitment is provisional and short-lived. They briefly align themselves with the author whose lines they speak and the company of which they are temporarily and arbitrarily a part. These brief assemblies of footloose young people are a breeding ground for sexual promiscuity, the condition which Sir Arnold deplores as 'the filth and degradation of our profession'. More fundamentally, the personal integrity of actors is constantly undermined by a professional life which invades the self, creating a duality at its core. This is the 'double life' of Cukor's film. Actors are both themselves and the parts they play – ego and alter-ego fused in the moment of performance. The process is appropriately dramatised in *The Flesh and Blood Show* when the distinction between the cuckolded Sir Arnold and the jealous Othello disappears, with lethal results. But the fusion of character and actor is even more explicit in exploitation performance when the script calls for a character to appear naked. In these circumstances it can only be the (usually female) actor's flesh which is exposed. However hard the actor might strive to create illusion, the flesh is real.

Beneath its Grand Guignol diegesis, *The Flesh and Blood Show* explores the relationship with real life and theatrical performance with all the insight and some of the erudition of a Dennis Potter play. Potter's key exploration of the theme, *Double Dare* (1976) would display remarkable affinities to Shaughnessy's screenplay, exhibiting a similar interest in the déjà vu phenomenon and constantly probing the relationship between the actor and the character portrayed.[25] Both texts are interested in the limits of performance and the consequences of the trend towards increasing verisimilitude in the theatrical display and use of the body. Where does the 'faking it' end and 'living it' begin?

Throughout *The Flesh and Blood Show*, there is constant reference to the ambiguous relationship between the real and the illusionary, between life and its imitation. Dummies are substituted for people; a man who seems to be dead is only sleeping; a woman who seems to be alive is 'really' dead, and so on. Not unusual pieces of trickery for a horror film, but uncommon in these quantities. The central motif which expresses this illusion of the fake-as-the-authentic is the macabre practical joke, a frequent element in the script. As Mike/Ray Brooks complains at one point, 'Somebody's having us on and I don't like it.' The theme is continued in the film's numerous plays within the play, in cinematographer Peter

Jessop's use of mirror images, and in a narrative structure which sets up fake killers (suspects) before revealing that the 'real' killer is a fake (that is, he is not who he pretends to be).

The real and the fake begin to function like the two images in the film's 3-D sequence. At first they seem distinct but the gaze fuses them together until the illusion is complete. At least, it would be complete if we were not also made acutely aware that the whole thing is a theatrical performance, by the self-consciously highlighted clichés of the whodunit and Simon/Robin Askwith's final declaration that 'if it wasn't so tragic and horrible it would almost make a movie script'. One might even say that as a simple genre text, the film itself is a fake, showing flesh and blood but concealing its more intellectual pretensions. Ultimately, of course, the 'somebody' who is 'having us on', the real practical joker, is the film-maker. He not only cons his audiences into thinking that what they see is real but, in this instance, he enjoys a kind of revenge on the acting profession of which he was once an undistinguished member. Not content with having his players denigrated as 'sex-crazed, evil and obscene young jackanapes', Peter Walker obliged them to suffer the privations of the flesh, scantily attired in a freezing location – or, as Sir Arnold puts it, 'Lashed naked to each other in a dark place where the sea doth rage below'.[26] Sir Arnold's jaundiced views on actors may well reflect some of Walker's own attitudes. His contempt for actors was noted by his regular scriptwriters, one of whom has reported Walker's complaint that 'all actors are egotistical poofs and all actresses are pompous prostitutes'.[27] Actors may be the butt of *The Flesh and Blood Show*'s jokes, but Walker at least shares in some of the humiliation, briefly stepping over the footlights to play an actor taking the part of Ludovico in a war-time production of *Othello*. He poses ironically as part of the great tradition of British stage drama.

The convolutions of its subtextual discourse on acting and illusion would, alone, be enough to redeem this rather slow and murky thriller, but there is much more here for the auteurist approaches to exploitation films. Many of Peter Walker's recurrent themes are very much in evidence here, notably permissiveness and the generation gap, the prison of the past and the degeneracy of the establishment. A permissive company of young actors naively assembles in one of those old dark places of English heritage, a decaying theatre.[28] They nickname this relic of another age 'The Morgue'. One character says it smells like an old museum, and beneath its stage are the rotting remains of its violent history, the illusionary violence of Grand Guignol production and the real violence of a war-time jealousy. As the story develops, the violent (British) past returns vindictively as a crazed patriarch with a knighthood that signifies the approval of an aged establishment. Interestingly, the one character who can control these atavistic emanations is the company's director (Ray Brooks) because only he understands the relationship between the past and the present. He can even offer, as we have seen, an explanation of déjà vu, the phenomenon of the past relived.

Brooks, as the director of the fictitious 'Flesh and Blood Show' seems to speak for Walker, the director of the 'real' *Flesh and Blood Show*. In explaining the character's fascination with macabre jokes, he inadvertently reveals a possible psychology of the horror film-maker: 'His morbid obsession with gruesome practical jokes is just a subconscious cloak to hide a dangerous obsession with violence. It's an outlet'.

Not only does *The Flesh and Blood Show* re-examine its director's favourite themes, but it also exhibits those autobiographic features which often characterise film auteurship. Peter Walker's childhood in Brighton was blighted by the death of his father, a successful comedian, and his desertion by his mentally disturbed mother. Walker sets his action at the time of his father's death in what was probably a key site of his childhood. His father, like Sir Arnold Gates, probably trod the boards of that same theatre at the end of the pier. In the celluloid fantasy, the lost father returns to join the child he abandoned 25 years before, and it is the faithless mother who remains dead. These parallels with personal biography add a surprising pathos to an apparently cynical exploitation venture.

We should now be able to see that, just as in the theatre in which it is set, there are a lot of strange things going on beneath the surface of *The Flesh and Blood Show*. Contrasting a public life with a subterranean parallel world is a typical Shaughnessy trope most clearly expressed in the title of his most successful project, *Upstairs, Downstairs,* and it is integral to the thematic structure of *The Flesh and Blood Show.* The film is a series of double exposures, which, as in its 3-D flashback sequence, offer to merge stereoscopically. We can schematically divide the film's binary oppositions into two overlapping groups, each with its own line of fracture through which opposites come together (see Table 5.1).

Table 5.1: Schematic of *The Flesh and Blood Show*

PRESENT		PAST	OPEN		HIDDEN
youth	/	old age	upstairs	/	downstairs
vitality	\	redundancy	auditorium	\	basement
company	/	Sir Arnold Gates	character	/	actor
of actors			action	\	motivation
victims	/	murderer	female body	/	male body
permissiveness	\	repression	diegesis	\	subtext
honesty	/	hypocrisy	appearance	/	reality
pop culture	\	high culture	on camera	\	behind the camera
			exploitation	/	art
cinema	\	theatre	narrative	\	film-maker's life
city	/	seaside	present	/	past
the audience	\	the film-makers			
open	/	hidden			

Line of fracture   Line of fracture

The Flesh and Blood Show demonstrates the possibilities of exploitation films as intellectually stimulating texts which might guardedly open themselves to the probing of their discursive practices. The film offers commentary on the director's emotional life, on the nature of performance, and even an attack on the privileged status of theatre in relation to cinema. Soon after its release George Perry wrote that 'within the British cultural establishment, the theatre is still regarded as superior to the film'.[29] Walker's film challenges this pre-eminence by representing the theatre as a decaying institution, poisoned by jealousy and presided over by a shameful cast of decadent actor-knights. But in its development of special effects and stereoscopic imagery, it shows, too, that if acting is illusion, then film is supreme in its ability to enhance that illusion.

The case of *The Flesh and Blood Show* suggests some important conclusions about cult and exploitation films and the ways in which they are understood both within and beyond the academy. First, that although interesting subtextual elements may enhance the reputation of exploitation films and give them 'a degree of respectability',[30] for most viewers they are unlikely to compensate for a lack of appeal in the more 'obvious' surface of the text. Thus, *The Flesh and Blood Show*'s failure to show much blood, its slow pace, predictable narrative and unexceptional looks militate against any further enquiry while the visual elan and narrative qualities of, say, *Peeping Tom* or *Night of the Living Dead* (1968) encourage subcutaneous investigation and cult canonisation. Second, we should be wary of dismissing cheap genre productions as 'paracinema', dumb sensationalism which can only be camply appreciated as 'bad film'. This is not, however, to say that movies like this, which exhibit a rich intellectual life and an apparent discrepancy between the audience addressed in their marketing and that implied by the complexity of their textuality, should be reclassified as 'art'. They were never intended to be taken seriously as profound artistic statements and any such pretensions would have alienated their intended audience. These movies were made as sensational entertainments by film-makers who either subconsciously expressed their own preoccupations or amused themselves by encoding their texts with encryptions that they never expected their audiences to decipher. As Murray Smith, another of Peter Walker's screenwriters, has remarked, his principal pleasure in writing for Walker was the freedom it gave him to get away with quietly mocking the hackneyed forms of popular melodrama and to include a series of droll in-jokes: 'I actually once said ... one day somebody's going to do a PhD on these movies and discover all those things that I put into them for fun.'[31]

Finally, to understand exploitation (or any other) films it is insufficient to simply read off textual characteristics, according to a predetermined theory of significance, as largely unconscious expressions of psychological and socio-political states. Instead, we must take seriously the personal as well as financial motivations of their creators, the cultural, social and economic conditions of their production and reception, and their audiences' responses both to a particular film as a spectacle and to its attempts to position them as spectators. This is a demanding task which has largely been rejected by academics and left to cinephiles outside the academy. This examination of *The Flesh and Blood Show* has left some areas unexplored and has only begun to point the way to a more fruitful historiography of exploitation cinema that may arise from a closer relationship between cinephiles and cinéastes.

Notes

1. Andrew Sarris, *The American Cinema: Directors and Directions 1929–68* (New York: Dutton, 1968), p. 24.
2. J. Hoberman and Jonathan Rosenbaum, *Midnight Movies* (New York: Harper and Row 1983), chs 2 and 3; Susan Sontag, 'Notes on camp', *Against Interpretation* (New York: Farrar Straus and Giroux, 1966).
3. Harry Medved and Michael Medved, *The Fifty Worst Movies of All Time* (New York: Popular Library ICBS, 1979) and *The Golden Turkey Awards* (New York: Pedigree, 1980).
4. Michael Weldon's *Psychotronic* magazine was first published in New York in 1980. With the help of other enthusiasts such as Bob Martin of *Fangoria* magazine, he was quickly able to assemble a reference work reviewing over 3000 movies: Michael Weldon, *The Psychotronic Encyclopedia of Film* (New York: Ballantine, 1983); John McCarty, *Splatter Movies* (Albany, New York: Fanta Co Enterprises Inc, 1981) and McCarty (ed.), *The Sleaze Merchants: Adventures in Exploitation Filmmaking* (New York: St Martin's Griffin, 1995); Danny Peary, *Cult Movies* (New York: Delta, 1981).
5. Jeffrey Sconce, 'Trashing the academy: taste, excess and the emerging politics of cinematic style', *Screen* 36, 4 (Winter 1995), pp. 371–93.
6. The significance of the shared cultural experience of the 'baby-boom' generation is powerfully argued in Fred Pfeil,

'Making flippy-floppy: postmodernism and the baby-boom PMC', *Another Tale To Tell: Politics and Narrative in Postmodern Culture* (London: Verso, 1990).

7. For a discussion of the relationships between cultural capital, autodidacticism and 'the new intellectuals' see Pierre Bourdieu, *Distinction: A Social Critique of the Judgement of Taste* (London: Routledge, 1989).

8. John Waters, *Shock Value: A Tasteful Book About Bad Taste* (New York: Dell, 1981), p. 192.

9. Both paradigms had their origins in different phases of the French journal *Cahiers du Cinéma*; Janet Staiger, 'The politics of film canons', *Cinema Journal* 24, 3 (Spring 1985), pp. 4–23.

10. See Mark Jancovich, *'Screen* theory', in Joanne Hollows and Mark Jancovich (eds), *Approaches to Popular Film* (Manchester: Manchester University Press, 1995), pp. 123–50.

11. Sconce, 'Trashing the academy', *passim.* See also Paul Watson, this volume.

12. David Docherty, David Morrison and Michael Tracey, *The Last Picture Show? Britain's Changing Film Audiences* (London: BFI, 1987), ch. 3.

13. Examples of 'instant' cult films include *Repo Man* (1983), *Liquid Sky* (1983) and *Heathers* (1989).

14. Welch Everman, *Cult Horror Films* (New York: Citadel, 1993).

15. William Schoell, *Stay Out of the Shower: The Shocker Film Phenomenon* (London: Robinson, 1988), ch. 9.

16. *The Flesh and Blood Show* was the first of Peter Walker's six 'terror' films. The others are *House of Whipcord* (1974), *Frightmare* (1974), *House of Mortal Sin* (1975), *Schizo* (1976) and *The Comeback* (1978). He once remarked:

> Horror is a word that I don't like to use because it has the connotations of Christopher Lee, Peter Cushing and fangs. The pictures I make – terror pictures I call them – are more identifiable. They have real people in unreal situations. Really what I'm trying to do is out-Hitchcock Hitchcock by putting a few more harder-hitting

ingredients into a picture that is rather vintage Hitchcock. (*Film Review* (April 1976), p. 36)

17. See, for example, the film's review in Phil Hardy (ed.), *The Aurum Film Encyclopedia: Horror* (London: Aurum 1985), p. 254.
18. Everyman, Hampstead: screened 28 May 1994 and reviewed in *Eurofest '94 Programme* (London: Media Publications, 1994). Phoenix Arts, Leicester: screened 1 October 1995 and reviewed in Steve Chibnall and I.Q. Hunter, *A Naughty Business: The British Cinema of Exploitation* (Leicester: De Montfort University, 1995).
19. The film took £13,060 in its first six weeks of release at London's Classic, Piccadilly Circus – a respectable sum for a low-budget exploitation film, but less than its predecessor, Walker's *Four Dimensions of Greta* (1972); Marjorie Bilbow, for example, patronisingly dismissed the film as suitable for 'uncritical younger audiences', *Cinema TV Today*, 4 November 1972.
20. J.P. Telotte, 'Beyond all reason: the nature of the cult', in J.P. Telotte (ed.), *The Cult Film Experience* (Austin: University of Texas, 1991), pp. 5–17.
21. Umberto Eco, 'Casablanca: cult movies and intertextual collage', *Travels in Hyperreality* (London: Picador, 1987), pp. 197–212.
22. Ibid., p. 212.
23. Both films are predated by *Men Are Not Gods* (1936), a British picture which also shows the problems of an actor playing Othello.
24. *The Flesh and Blood Show*'s American distributor, David Friedman, had deconstructed the sexploitation movie in his *Starlet* (1969).
25. Potter's play examines a male writer's fantasies about an actress who is being cast as a prostitute. While she thinks of acting as 'the opposite of being yourself', he struggles to disassociate 'private acts and emotions' from 'public performance' because the same body experiences, or is responsible, for both. Prostitutes become actresses when they simulate emotion, but do actresses becomes

prostitutes when they engage in sexual acts as part of a role?

> Actress: The I that is me and the I that is the character
> – whore/actress – they get mixed up. One being me,
> and the other being a whore which is also me – which,
> let's face it, is still the way – the secret, half-hidden
> sneaky way – that writers, directors and even audiences
> want to think about actresses like me.

26. See location report on *The Flesh and Blood Show*, *Cinema Rising*, May 1972.
27. David McGillivray, 'Spawn of *Tarantula!*: a career in British sleaze' in Stefan Jaworzyn (ed.), *Shock Express* (London: Titan, 1992), pp. 126–33.
28. For a discussion of the role of heritage locations in British horror films, see I.Q. Hunter, 'Deadly manors: the country house in British exploitation films' in Paul Cooke, David Sadler and Nicholas Zurbrugg (eds), *Locating Identity: Essays on Nation, Community and the Self* (Leicester: De Montfort University, 1996), pp. 45–55.
29. George Perry, *The Great British Picture Show* (London: Paladin, 1975), p. 11.
30. Barry K. Grant, 'Science fiction double feature', in Telotte, *Cult Film Experience*, pp. 122–37.
31. Interview with Murray Smith, 2 June 1996.

6

Faecal Phantoms: Oral and Anal Tensions in *The Tingler*

Mikita Brottman

Ladies and Gentlemen, there is no need to be alarmed ... Please remain seated. The movie will begin right away. I repeat, there is no cause for alarm ...[1]

William Castle is probably best remembered as the director of a series of low-budget horror films made between 1958 and 1962, for it was in these successful but exploitative chillers that he formed a personal bond with his audience through a wide series of ingenious, carnival-style gimmicks and hokum gimcracks. Early experiments with widescreen 3-D features and on-camera appearances (to introduce himself and to prepare the audience for the forthcoming cinematic experience) led Castle to the invention of various promotional ploys and exploitation devices that guaranteed his films their inevitable box-office success. 'I've modelled my career on P.T. Barnum', he once boasted, and his influence on the subsequent history of exploitation cinema is undeniable. John Waters, the inventor of 'Odorama', has referred to Castle as 'King of the Gimmicks', confessing that 'William Castle was my idol. His films made me want to make films. I'm even jealous of his work. In fact, I wish I *were* William Castle.'[2]

The first of these carnivalesque cinematic experiences came with the release of *Macabre* in early 1958, for which Castle took out a policy with Lloyds of London insuring every ticket buyer for $1000 in case they died from fright. Mock insurance policies appeared in all the newspaper ads. Giant replicas of the actual policy hung over the marquees. Hearses were parked outside the theatres, fake nurses in uniform were paid to stand around the lobbies, and Castle himself even arrived in a hearse at some of the film's premieres, and made his entrance emerging from a coffin. *Macabre* was followed up in the autumn of the same year with *The House on Haunted Hill*, featuring an intriguing new slant on the recently-deceased 3-D process which Castle named 'Emergo'. Theatres showcasing *The House on Haunted Hill* were wired from screen to balcony with a pair of cables. At a climactic moment in the film, the screen momentarily blackens, cueing the projectionist to set in motion a 12-foot illuminated plastic skeleton which, in the words of the *New York Times* movie reviewer, 'slid straight forward to the balcony, blankly eyed the first row customers, and slid back'.[3] The luminous skeleton upstaged even Vincent Price, Castle's first real star, especially – as often seems to have happened – if it got stuck half way down its cables or if the skeleton jumped its wires completely and fell into the audience, causing hysterical frenzy.[4]

Thirteen Ghosts in 1960 offered its enthusiastic audience the experimental device of 'Illusion-O', where each spectator was presented with a 'ghost viewer', an obscure twist on 3-D glasses. The 'ghost viewer' extended Castle's promotional fascination with audience participation – one half of the 'ghost viewer' allowed the spectator to see the thirteen ghosts, and the other half didn't, leaving the film blurred and surreal. Waters remembers that, while audiences seemed 'bewildered' by this rather imperfect technical breakthrough, 'they still bought the gimmick'.[5] *Thirteen Ghosts* was followed up by the transvestite-themed shocker, *Homicidal* (1961), heavily influenced by Hitchcock's *Psycho* (1960), during whose screening cinemas refused admission after the film had already begun. *Homicidal* featured a 'fright break' two minutes before the end of the film, during which time the screen would go blank and Castle's voice, backed by the sound of a heartbeat, would announce that anyone too frightened to watch the end of the film could leave the theatre and their full admission charge refunded. In a number of cinemas, those leaving the film during the 'fright break' had to follow yellow footsteps up the aisle, bathed in a yellow light, past yellow lines with the stencilled message 'Cowards Keep Walking', past a nurse who would offer a blood pressure test, to a yellow cardboard booth in the lobby called 'Coward's Corner', where, to the accompaniment of a record blaring 'Watch the chicken! Watch him shiver in Coward's Corner!', he would be forced to sign a yellow card stating that 'I am a *bona fide* coward'. Different coloured tickets were issued for each show, so the audience could not sit through the film twice and leave during the second 'fright break' to get their admission refunded.[6]

Homicidal was followed up in the same year with *Mr Sardonicus*, featuring the 'Punishment Poll'. On entering the theatre, the spectator was issued with a dayglow card containing a thumbs up/thumbs down design similar to a playing card. Before the last reel of the film, an usher conducted the Punishment Poll and the audience was allowed to determine the fate of Mr Sardonicus by holding up their Mercy/No Mercy verdicts to be counted. Although Castle supplied every print of the film with two different endings, Waters claims that 'not *once* did an audience grant mercy, so this one particular part of the film has *never* been seen'.[7] Castle's next film, *Zotz!* (1962) was accompanied by the creation of millions of magic 'Zotz' coins, distributed weeks in advance of the film's release to guarantee promotional success, and *13 Frightened Girls* (1963) was promoted with the gimmick of a worldwide talent hunt for the prettiest girl in each of thirteen countries who, when cast, would receive $300, hotel accommodation and a 'first class' new wardrobe. *Straightjacket* (1963), with Joan Crawford, included free gifts of small cardboard axes streaked with simulated blood, and in Castle's final gimmick, for all showings of *I Saw What You Did* (1965), the back three rows of the cinema were advertised as the 'shock section' and fitted out with seatbelts on each chair to prevent the spectator being jolted out of fear.

The most ambitious and radical experiment in audience participation, however, was without a doubt Castle's device of 'Percepto', installed to accompany all cinema screenings of *The Tingler* (1959), featuring Vincent Price as Dr Warren Chapin, a research scientist deeply engaged in experimentation on the cause and often lethal effects of human fear. Chapin suspects that many people who have died from extreme fear were killed by a parasite that takes shape within the vertebrae – 'the tingler' – which can be prevented from materialising only by the victim's screams. If a person is not able to release this tension, however, the 'tingler' takes shape and cracks the human spine.

Having removed the insectoid creature from the spine of one of its victims, the tingler escapes from Chapin, slips down under the floorboards and makes its way into a silent movie theatre beneath the flat. Here, it attacks a girl in the audience, causing widespread hysterics. Dr Chapin's voice is heard on the darkened screen assuring the audience that the girl is being taken care of and that everything is under control. Moments later, a second tingler attack takes place, this time on the projectionist. The lights dim again, and the projected silhouette of the tingler crawls across the cinema screen. Chapin addresses the audience once more, this time to encourage everyone to 'Scream for your lives!' until the tingler is paralysed, the danger has passed and 'We can now return to our picture'.

Percepto involved small electric motors, similar to handshake buzzers, wired up to a certain number of cinema seats. In the film, when the tingler breaks loose in the movie theatre and kills the projectionist, the screen would go blank and a voice would announce: 'Attention! The tingler is loose in this theatre. Please scream for your life.' At this point, a specially planted female stooge in the audience would burst into hysterics and have to be carried out by a nurse in uniform. Moments later, during the second tingler attack, the projectionist would push a button activating the electrical charges on the wired-up cinema seats, allowing certain spectators to be hit at the base of the spine by a brief electrical jolt. The screen dims again, and Dr Chapin encourages the cinema audience to 'scream for your lives', echoed by the pandemonium of the on-screen cinema audience screaming lines like: 'It's over here! Help! It's over here!' Ideally, the *real* audience were literally swept into the film's action by the buzzing of the Percepto activators, until Chapin assures the audience that the tingler has been paralysed, the danger has passed, and 'We will now return to our picture'.

Like Emergo, Percepto did not always function as the director might have anticipated. The most common anecdote, recounted by Castle in his autobiography *Step Right Up!*, involved a cinema whose management, having dutifully installed the Percepto equipment the night before *The Tingler*

was supposed to be shown, decided to test the device on a group
of older women who were watching *The Nun's Story* on the last
night of its run, with predictably hysterical results.[8] Waters tells
an anecdote about a showing in Philadelphia where one beefy
truck driver was so incensed by the Percepto buzzer underneath
his chair that he ripped his entire seat from the floor, and had
to be subdued by five ushers.[9] Other Castle fans remember their
suspense being broken by a broadcast announcement that
'The tingler is wanted in the lobby'. John Waters describes his
experience of *The Tingler* as 'the fondest movie-going memory
of my youth':

> I went to see it every day. Since, by the time it came to my
> neighbourhood, only about ten random seats were wired,
> I would run through the theatre searching for the magic
> buzzers. As I sat there experiencing the miracle of Percepto,
> I realised there could be such a thing as Art in the cinema.[10]

While Castle's deployment of experimental audience-
participation devices was directed wholly towards promotional
ends, *The Tingler* is in fact a deeply complex and interesting
film, and in wiring up his cinema seats with electrical cables,
Castle was actually – albeit unknowingly – extending the
principles of experimentation with theatre, audience and
spectacle first devised by the Italian Futurist movement in the
late 1920s. A reading which attends to these complexities,
however, tends to meet a great deal of resistance from critics
and fans of the exploitation film, most of whom would argue
that *The Tingler* is a piece of hokum whose sheer effrontery is
enjoyable in itself, that Castle's sole priority was to entertain,
and that, as critic John Brunas comments in *Midnight Marquee*,
'to search deeper into [Castle's] productions for obscure
messages is critical pretentiousness of the first order'.[11] Most
critics of the exploitation film unhesitatingly write off Castle's
films as unadulterated schlock – a brand of suspense that is
thoroughly unsubtle, relying on a surface facetiousness and
tongue-in-cheek aplomb enlivened by moments of sudden,
shrill shock.

These are certainly all characteristics of Castle's films, of
which *The Tingler* is the most tricksy and hokum-laden

example. But it seems strange that critics like Brunas find it paradoxical that a piece of cinematic spectacle devised wholly for commercial ends should contain a 'deeper' level of symbolic themes and meditations, especially if they are encoded in the unconscious of the cinematic text. One of the most important aims of film criticism is to concretise and vivify the symbolic nature of these half-thoughts and semi-awarenesses that the plot of the film makes manifest, however superficially, sporadically or facetiously. Interestingly enough, in an interview with *Cinefantastique* less than two years before his death, Castle remarked on his fascination with contemporary theoretical analysis of his 1950s and 1960s horror films, which, as Castle points out, 'are being treated with increasing respect, and taken very seriously today at the universities where they study them'.[12] He goes on to make some other observations:

> It's a very strange thing. I definitely feel that possibly in my unconscious I was trying to say something ... I never expected that they would put under a microscope pictures that I made in the fifties and sixties and look for hidden meanings. Nevertheless, that is what is happening ... And I think about inner meaning, truly, it is possible that deeply buried within my unconscious was the feeling of trying to say something ... And I get this from *The Tingler*.[13]

The tendency to take Castle's films seriously is clearly not widespread enough for John Waters, whose retrospective of Castle's work in *American Film* is in part an attack on critics for being slow to elevate 'this ultimate eccentric director-producer' to cult status ('Isn't it time for a retrospective? A documentary on his life? Some highfalutin critique in *Cahiers du Cinéma*? ... Forget Ed Wood. Forget George Romero. William Castle was best. William Castle was God').[14] In fact, uncharacteristically, Waters was behind the times. *Cahiers du Cinéma* had published a long article about Castle's work by way of obituary on his death in 1977, remarking on some of the ways in which films like *The Tingler* stand as realisations of the spectacular 'happening-cinema' conceived by the Futurist movement: a system of traumatisation, 'where the spectacle unfolds not only on the screen, but also in the room, with special effects that allowed the audience to be played with like puppets ... Even the spectator who remains glued to his seat is nevertheless involved. The effects stopped at nothing.'[15] Comparing Castle's work to that of Italian horror auteur Dario Argento, *Cahiers du Cinéma* praises *The Tingler* for its innovative use of the colour red for shock sequences (in an otherwise black-and-white film), describing the film as 'unfolding at the limits of psychodrama', and 'in the popular psychoanalytic style of Tennessee Williams'. For Castle, it concludes, 'only the spectacle counted'.[16]

As Robert Musil observes in *The Man Without Qualities*, 'The moment one begins to take a serious interest in anything, no matter how ludicrous or lacking in aesthetic sense, and puts it on an equality with other things, it begins to reveal a harmonious order of its own, to give off the intoxicating scent of its own self love, its indwelling urge to play and be liked.'[17] It is interesting that a whole spectrum of established film critics, from the eccentric (John Waters in *American Film*) to the sober (Howard Gensler in *Premiere*) have recalled a childhood experience of *The Tingler* as their archetypal horror movie-going experience, and it has long been a commonplace of horror film criticism – ever since the publication of Robin Wood's 'An Introduction to the American Horror Film' in 1979 – that such experiences can be far more profound than those available to spectators of more 'serious' cinema.[18]

John Fraser catalogues some of the more marvellous aspects of horror movies which help to realise this complexity of emotional experience. First, according to Fraser, there is the marvellousness of the supernatural, or of things and events so exotic as to border on the supernatural, such as the notion of a crustacean parasite existing along the human spine, energised and given strength by the emotion of human fear, which brings it to life as a separate, living thing. Second, there are the surrealistic creations of the imaginations of non-supernatural characters, such as Dr Chapin's baroque laboratory with its skulls and skeletons, its cats and dogs in cages, or Olly's shady home, built on top of a silent movie theatre ('It's kind of old-fashioned, but [Martha] likes it that way', says Olly of his gloomy house). Third, normal-seeming people reveal horrendous qualities.[19] The dedicated research scientist becomes an ingenious loon, willing to threaten his wife with a gun and frighten a deaf-mute to death in a deluded attempt to infringe the essential principles of nature, just as the mild and lowly Olly is unmasked as an avaricious wife-killer. Everyday objects become charged with great menace, such as the teacup Chapin smashes and uses as a weapon with which to draw his own blood, questioning the extent of Martha's obsessive-compulsive affliction (she washes her hands constantly, opens up the safe and counts her money again and again, and the sight of just a small drop of blood causes her to tense, panic and faint).

Environments intended to be nurturing become very much the opposite in *The Tingler*, like Chapin's Regency mansion or the silent movie theatre where the tingler is accidentally let loose. In the same way, seemingly immutable social or vocational occasions are likewise fearsomely desanctified, such as the gentle Dr Chapin's home visit to his patient Martha Higgins, or Chapin and his wife drinking a toast to celebrate the success of his latest scientific discovery ('Here's to the tingler!'). And other habitually familiar scenarios are disrupted: a doctor giving his patient a ride home turns into an experiment in the pathology of human fear; a deaf-mute woman's paranoia gives rise to a horrifying series of shocks resulting in her death by fright. Most fundamental to the horror movie gestalt, however, is *The Tingler*'s classic narrative projection of a progressive entry into a forbidden centre. This centre is Chapin's laboratory, with its skeletons, corpses, caged animals and hallucinogenic potions, symbolising Chapin's desperate desire to *find out*, and the possible dangers of doing so. Dave's stolen dogs and cats are rejected by Chapin in favour of self-experimentation. 'I want to personally sense the power of the tingler in a controlled fear situation', he claims, 'but nothing scares me'. And yet as Warren later says to Dave, 'To break the laws of nature is a dangerous thing, and we've not only broken its laws, we've violated its basic principles. We had to, and now we've got to stop.' Or, in the words of that old horror movie motif: 'There are some things man was not meant to know.'

With respect to the fascination laid bare in *The Tingler* with the physiology of the human body – both the on-screen bodies, and the participating bodies of the cinema audience – it seems most appropriate to use an anthropological paradigm in order to gain access to the film's conscious and unconscious implications. Anthropology is also significant because it allows the critic to negotiate Castle's understanding of the ancient commonality of the human body, its failings, ruptures and weaknesses.

The pattern that starts to emerge from a close analysis of *The Tingler* is one which makes known the close relationship between the symbolic and the social order, disclosing how each gives form to the other in a dynamic intermingling of meanings. A careful analysis of this film is not only a theoretical exercise in cinema studies, but a way of understanding the history of human cultures, and the symbolic importance of their narratives. To chart analogues between the symbol structure of contemporary narratives and the belief systems of earlier societies is not, as it may first seem, an attempt to cast a net further and wider for similar cultural paradigms, but rather an effort to look more deeply at the history of the human body, with its secret and disguised level of conscious understanding. For example, a number of primitive cultures such as the Navajo and the Mandari also tell narratives like that of *The Tingler,* involving versions of the 'animal double' motif. Some societies even accept it as a matter of certainty that many people have wild beasts like the tingler inside their bodies. These are either people with the power to temporarily assume the form of an animal, or animals that can assume a human form.[20]

The traditional animal double inhabits ambiguous areas of the social domain, habitually presiding at funerals and ghost sacrifices. It has been suggested by anthropologists such as Halverson, Buxton and Loudon[21] that the animal double presides over areas of social and cultural life which are by nature ambiguous, unpredictable and dangerous. Similarly, the tingler is associated with murders, autopsies and funerals as well as the nether worlds of neurosis, paranoia and mistrust and the ambiguous domains of death and sex, in the context of which such social concepts as marriage, money, punishment and desire must be negotiated. Like the more traditional animal doubles, the tingler presides over a night-world of psychosis, adultery, theft, bribery, corruption, broken promises, broken marriages and wife-murder.

One final point on this theme. The animal double does not always take the form of an *animal* (in the zoological sense); it may equally take the form of an insect, fish or bird. The tingler is a kind of hybrid parasite – a cross between a worm, a lobster and a centipede. Castle describes it in his autobiography as 'sort of like a lobster, but flat, and instead of claws it has long, slimy feelers'. While there are plenty of examples of animal doubles that take the form of shellfish or insects, it is worth examining the fact that these categories of creatures are in themselves ambiguous and liminal. Shellfish, reptiles and insects are the equivocal residue of the animal world, not quite animals and not quite fish, considered by some cultures to be the evil enemies of mankind.[22] Anthropologists such as Bleek, Halverson and (most famously) Levi-Strauss (in *The Raw and the Cooked*)[23] have suggested that insects are considered abject and interstitial because they are not rated as food, in most countries at least, whereas reptiles and shellfish are determined to be freakish and ambiguous because their cold-bloodedness distances them from our far greater affective closeness to warm-blooded animals and birds. In this light, it is somewhat ironic that insects, reptiles and shellfish are referenced metaphorically in many societies to describe the kind of witchcraft accusations that occur within a domestic situation, where people all live closely together, as in the Kwahu proverb 'Only the insect in your own cloth will bite you'.[24]

Interestingly, a number of primitive and tribal cultures conceive of the animal double as faecal in form and consistency.[25] If the province of this creation is to negotiate those ambiguous areas of culture and social structure, it is wholly fitting that the animal double should emerge from the indistinct boundaries of the human body. In direct opposition to everything we consider human, the animal is a category inhabiting all those dark, shadowy crevices of human culture and the human body: not inside but outside, not the womb but the anus, not birth but defecation. There is obviously something faecal about the tingler. It is a worm-like protuberance that gradually emerges from the anal inner space, accompanied by a range of physical perceptions and sensations both pleasant and disturbing. The emergence of the tingler involves agonised writhings, expressions of pain, groans and wrenching sounds followed by the sudden expulsion of an object from within the lower body.

Yet in this story, the ability to produce human sound prevents the emergence of this faecal beast from the anal space. The faecal animal, 'the force that makes your spine tingle when you're scared', has somehow transformed itself into a human voice. The metapsychology of the inner space of the human body image is so complex and multifaceted that it allows ample opportunity for cathexis, both concrete and symbolic, between different bodily openings, inner spaces, and the contents hidden behind these openings. In fact, the entire structural foundation for the inner body image is created by the effect of various sensations and actual functions of the body simultaneously with phase-specific images and figures of speech that are connected with the body.[26]

So, for instance, the sound of the human voice can easily be imaginatively experienced as faeces, flatus or urination – especially in cases of psychosis where the image of the body, especially its inner space, is disturbed. In relation to the top half of the inner body image, the lungs, larynx and ears compose an inner space entity, the 'excrement' or product of which is the human voice, words and sounds – we react to important experiences by taking a deep breath, as though to internalise the auditory experience better, and our reaction to experiences we dislike or despise often involves expiration. Thus, in relation to the metapsychology of the human body image, it seems quite natural that a faecal image from the anus should be cathected into the inner space of the human voice.

The basic notion of the tingler is of a parasite that feeds off the stress and tension experienced in the spinal column at moments of intense fear. This tension can be released only by screaming which, in turn, cuts off the tingler from its source of strength and renders it powerless. Scream, and you are safe. Fail to scream, and your body is lost to the tingler. When Dr Chapin exhorts the on-screen audience to 'Scream for your lives!' to disempower the escaped tingler, he is also encouraging the screams of the by now hysterical *actual* cinema audience, whose panic-stricken reaction to random jolts of electrical energy should ideally, at least according to Castle's plan, serve as a promotional device to entice the crowds waiting in the lobby in for the next showing.

Put in its most simple terms, the human fear of losing control of one's defecatory functions – embodied by the sight of an enormous, swollen faecal animal, alive and on the loose – is cathected into the socially legitimate chaos of ritual screaming (itself inspired by the screams of the on-screen cinema audience). As I suggested earlier, uncontrolled defecation and an ungovernable vocal spasm are essentially different manifestations of the same bodily impulse, the significant difference being that chaotic defecation is considered horrific and polluting, whereas ungovernable screaming fits into a legitimate social category, and has a communally accepted social function. To view *The Tingler*, as it was originally screened, is therefore to take part in a socially endorsed ritual of cathexis, where the threat of contamination is faced head-on, displaced and overcome. And for those audience members fortunate enough to select seats rigged up with Percepto-buzzers directing an electrical jolt underneath the buttocks, the experience can only have been doubly exciting and doubly hysterical, impelling the leading voices in the train of screams to follow. The dynamics of this socialisation procedure make it easy to understand, perhaps, why memories of going to watch *The Tingler* are recalled by so many film writers and critics as the most intense and exhilarating movie-going experience of their youth.

The Tingler is a tale of warning. It is a story of assault by a faecal animal double which comes to life inside the body at the peak of terror, extending 'from the coccyx to the sternum', and when released outside the body takes on a life of its own and crawls around frantically, causing a violent anal jolt when it attacks. This faecal creation is the product of massive unreleased tension, and can be calmed only by the cathexis of this defecatory neurosis into the vocal release of the scream. On one level then, this is a film about what Philip Rieff has described as 'the triumph of the therapeutic',[27] a trait of which is the widely-held belief – almost a commonplace by 1959 – that emotions we fail to get 'out' somehow remain repressed 'within' us until they find their own way 'out', possibly of their own accord, and possibly in a rather frightening and hazardous way. The popular secularisation of Freudian psychoanalysis allows for the expression of certain kinds of so-called 'repressed desires and urges' to become increasingly acceptable in the name of a process of psychic cleansing, with certain kinds of desires and urges, such as homosexuality, fetishism and transvestism, remaining far more permissible than others. As it has become increasingly common over the last 30 years to attribute such repressed complexes to triggering childhood events – usually sexual or emotionally abusive parenting – the disclosure and display of such drives has met increasing approval.

But *The Tingler* is a more involved film than a reading based on this therapeutic model might suggest. This is not a film about the expression of repressed fears in a tension-breaking psychic catharsis. Because it cannot be 'attributed' to an early triggering event, because it will never become socially acceptable and because its effect is universal, the defecatory obsession is not really a neurosis we can 'get in touch' with, 'come to terms' with, like other unconscious urges. Horror at the perverseness of our bodily emissions is not just a repressed impulse waiting to return, but part of the neurological disease of being human. *The Tingler* is a bodily nightmare in which a faecal animal, swollen to grotesque proportions, is given a life of its own and let loose upon the unsuspecting world of consciousness. The plight of an unfortunate neurotic deaf-mute whose unreleased tensions grow so great that they overcome her is simply the signal impelling the process of cathexis in the cinema audience from anal neurosis to oral expulsion, and back again. Contrary to therapeutic fashion, however, this cathexis neither alleviates nor endures. The relief expressed in the scream of the spectator is nothing more than a socially admissible ritual of momentary release. In Castle's fantasy, the scream destroys the neurosis. But in the waking reality of our bodily lives, the defecatory obsession, like the faecal process itself, like all the best monsters, is totally indestructible.

Notes

1. Dr Chapin (Vincent Price) reassures the terrified silent movie audience in William Castle's *The Tingler* (1959).

2. John Waters, 'Whatever happened to showmanship?', *American Film* 9 (December 1983), pp. 55–8.
3. John Brunas, 'William Castle: five portraits in black (1958–61)', *Midnight Marquee* 29 (September 1979), p. 7.
4. See Waters, 'Whatever happened to showmanship?', p. 56, and Bill Burgess, 'William Castle', *Classic Images* 111 (September 1984), pp. 42–4.
5. Waters, 'Whatever happened to showmanship?', p. 57.
6. Ibid.
7. Ibid., p. 58.
8. William Castle, *Step Right Up! I'm Gonna Scare the Pants off America* (New York: Putnam's Sons, 1976), p. 132.
9. Waters, 'Whatever happened to showmanship?', p. 57.
10. Ibid.
11. Brunas, 'William Castle', p. 4.
12. Daniel P. Scaperotti, 'The horror of personality directors: Castle', *Cinefantastique* 3.3 (September 1975), p. 20.
13. Ibid.
14. Waters, 'Whatever happened to showmanship?', p. 57.
15. Alain Garel, 'William Castle' (obituary), *Cahiers du Cinéma* 21 (1977), pp. 70–1.
16. Ibid.
17. Robert Musil, *The Man Without Qualities*, trans. Eithne Watkins and Ernst Kaiser, vol. III (London: Pandora, 1979), p. 321.
18. Howard Gensler, 'Terror of the Tingler', *Premiere* (US), (May 1993), p. 89, Robin Wood, 'An introduction to the American horror film', in Andrew Britton et al. (eds), *American Nightmare: Essays on the Horror Film* (Toronto: Festival of Festivals, 1979), pp. 10–35, reprinted in Bill Nichols (ed.), *Movies and Methods* (Berkeley: University of California Press, 1989), vol. 2, pp. 195–220.
19. John Fraser, 'Watching horror movies', *Michigan Quarterly Review* 16, 1 (1990), pp. 39–54.
20. See Jean Buxton, 'Animal identity and human peril: some Mandari images', *Man* 3, 1 (1968), pp. 35–50, and Peggy E. Alford, 'Anglo-American perceptions of Navajo skinwalker legends', *Contemporary Legend* 2 (1992), pp. 119–36.

21. John B. Loudon, 'On body products', in John Blacking (ed.), *The Anthropology of the Body*, proceedings of the Association of Social Anthropologists of the Commonwealth Conference on the Anthropology of the Body (Belfast: Academic Press, 1975), pp. 94–109.
22. John Halverson, 'Animal categories and terms of abuse', *Man* 11, 4 (1976), pp. 503–25.
23. Claude Levi-Strauss, *The Raw and the Cooked: Introduction to a Science of Mythology* (London: Penguin, 1992).
24. Wolf Bleek, 'Witchcraft, gossip and death: a social drama', *Man* 11, 4 (1976), pp. 526–42.
25. Cultures that conceive of the animal double as faecal include the Melanesians, discussed in F. Panoff, 'Food and faeces: a Melanesian rite', *Man* 5, 2 (1970), pp. 237–53, and the Jivaro, discussed in Martin Horner, 'Jivaro souls', *American Anthropologist* 64 (1962), pp. 258–72.
26. Tor-Björn Hägglund and Piha Heikki, 'The inner space of the body image', *Psychoanalytic Quarterly* 49 (1980), pp. 256–83.
27. Philip Rieff, *The Triumph of the Therapeutic: Uses of Faith After Freud* (New York: University of Chicago Press, 1966).

7

Seducing the Subject: Freddy Krueger, Popular Culture and the *Nightmare on Elm Street* Films

Ian Conrich

The *A Nightmare on Elm Street* films have been an extremely successful series. A 1991 press release from the American producers, New Line, reported that the first five of the seven films had taken over $400 million from the domestic and foreign box office, video cassette sales, television and merchandising. *Variety* has recorded the productions as among the most profitable of horror films in terms of film rentals at theatres in the US and Canada. The first film in the series, *A Nightmare on Elm Street* (1984), directed by Wes Craven, has receipts of $9,337,942. *A Nightmare on Elm Street Part 2: Freddy's Revenge* (1985), directed by Jack Sholder, has receipts of $13,500,000, while receipts of $21,345,000 have been recorded for *A Nightmare on Elm Street Part 3: The Dream Warriors* (1987), directed by Chuck Russell. *A Nightmare on Elm Street Part 4: The Dream Master* (1988), directed by Renny Harlin, recorded receipts of $22,000,000. *A Nightmare on Elm Street Part 5: The Dream Child* (1989), directed by Stephen Hopkins, took $10,000,000 and *Freddy's Dead: The Final Nightmare* (1991), directed by Rachel Talalay, took $17,700,000. *Wes Craven's New Nightmare* (Part 7) was released in 1994.[1]

These figures reflect, on one level, the cultural impact of the *Nightmare* films. The marketing of Freddy Krueger and the merchandising associated with the series established the films, particularly in the late 1980s, as a popular culture phenomenon. It is, however, not so much the success of the films that is surprising, but the fact that they featured a child-killer as their protagonist. The *Nightmare* films depict the

118

activities of Freddy Krueger, a child molester and murderer, who, having escaped conviction on a technicality, was burnt to death in his boiler room by Elm Street's vengeful parents. Years later he returns, initially through the dreams of the teenage children of the parents who destroyed him, later through the dreams of all children living in the Elm Street area. Here, as the teenagers are tormented and killed, Freddy ruptures the boundaries between the imaginary and the real. The *Nightmare* films have been largely successful through their ability to maintain a seduction of the subject, that is of the spectator and consumer. This has predominantly been achieved through Freddy, the cultural object, who seduces the subject through a combination of his power and personality and a supporting series of clever images and stimulating visuals. This seduction continues with the associated merchandising, where popular culture allows for the successful release of Freddy from the fictional world of the film into a consumer society reality.[2]

Freddy Krueger has a very recognisable identity: a red-and-green horizontally striped jumper, a razors-for-fingers glove, a fedora hat and, in the words of Robert Englund, the actor who plays him, 'a Cagney swagger and a cool-clown style'.[3] His appearances are frequently marked by a maniacal laugh and the screeching of his razor-blade fingers on metal. In contrast, the other characters in the films possess weak identities. While Freddy is the 'fixed' element in the *Nightmare* series, his various victims are easily interchangeable. Freddy's identity is so strong that it can absorb the images of his victims. In *Nightmare 2*, Jesse, possessed by Freddy's spirit, ceases to be the Jesse that his friends and parents know and slowly begins to display parts of Freddy's identity. Jesse's hand transforms into Freddy's razors-for-fingers gloved hand, and, while kissing his girlfriend, he sprouts an enormous Freddy tongue. Eventually, a complete Freddy emerges from within Jesse's stomach, leaving Jesse's empty body to fall to the ground. In *Nightmare 5*, Freddy's victims are presented as sperm-shaped expulsions that erupt from his body when he is destroyed in the film's conclusion. Similarly *Nightmare 4* presents the trapped victims as little outlines of human forms frantically pushing at the surface of Freddy's torso from inside; the faces of recent victims screaming in pain, pushing against the membrane that traps them within Freddy's body.

Capable of transforming into almost anything, anytime, anywhere, Freddy possesses a tremendous power to surprise and entertain. As Henry Jenkins has observed,

> We face the challenge of Freddy's shape-shifting as he moves between different cultural categories – male and female, adult and child, animate and inanimate, takes control over domestic technologies, assumes identities from mass culture, mutates and disintegrates before our eyes, only to be reconfigured and re-embodied again.[4]

In *Nightmare 5*, he is both a diving board that attempts to curl itself around a diver, and a motorbike which penetrates and physically merges with the body of its passenger. In an earlier film, *Nightmare 3*, he becomes a giant snake that attempts to swallow a girl whole, and appears as an attractive nurse that seduces a boy.

Possessing the ability to destroy the individuals through their dreams, Freddy functions as the personification of the ultimate nightmare. Frequently attacking his victims through their weaknesses, his methods are astounding and ingenious. In *Nightmare 4*, a teenager with an abhorrence for cockroaches is herself dramatically transformed in a Kafkaesque fashion into a cockroach, which Freddy then crushes with his foot. A girl who observes a strict diet is force-fed to death by Freddy in *Nightmare 5*, while in *Nightmare 3* an ex-drug addict is lethally injected through ten needles emerging from Freddy's fingers. These elaborate special effects are of such importance to the films that they are awarded lengthy end credits. Their technicians are grouped into teams of 'operators' that have an average of six members, with the spectacles each given an individual descriptive title, such as 'Dan's Mechanical Suit/Freddy Bike' and 'Womb with a View/Fetal Canal' in *Nightmare 5*. The special effects dominate the series to such an extent that frequently spectators describing a *Nightmare* film will only mention the spectacular moments: the human puppet in *Nightmare 3* or the explosion of the deaf boy's head in

Nightmare 6. Jeffrey Sconce has described these repeated moments as 'episodes of intense visual excitement', suggesting that they are one reason why the *Nightmare* films have proved so popular with a youth audience.[5] Recent 'kid culture' has been attracted to the spectacle as entertainment, where a rapid succession of perceptual information subverts the importance of the plot – a kind of visual stimulation manifested in many highly addictive video games.

The special effects employed in the films are spectacles that function around the appearance and performance of Freddy. As the dominant image, in narratives dependent on an episodic structure, Freddy's appearance signals the next series of outrageous and spectacular effects. As David Edelstein writes in the *Village Voice*, 'The dreams are big production numbers and Freddy presides over them like a nightclub master-of-ceremonies.'[6] Other popular horror figures in contemporary films have tended to be faceless and devoid of personality. Monstrous characters such as Jason Voorhees of the *Friday the 13th* series, Leatherface of *The Texas Chainsaw Massacre* films and *Halloween*'s Michael Myers are deadly but mechanical and silent, with the films structured upon a series of repetitive and predictable killings.

By contrast, Freddy is the confident performer, the host, the showman and the comic. He is ostentatious, 'courteous', even courtly and is constantly cracking jokes. In *Nightmare 3*, when Nancy demands that Freddy release Joey, Freddy declares, 'Your wish is my command!' and walks backwards away from Joey, his arms outstretched and his hat held in his right hand. Here he looks like an Elizabethan gentleman, his manner both accommodating and full of pomp. In *Nightmare 4* one sequence has a girl dreaming that she is on the beach of an exotic island, when Freddy appears through an exploding sand-castle. Having made his grand entrance, Freddy walks towards his new victim, smiles and puts on a pair of sunglasses. His arrival is spectacular, his manner smooth – so smooth that he even gets to rap the song 'Are You Ready for Freddy?' with 'The Fat Boys' over the film's end credits. As Henry Jenkins writes: 'Freddy moves through the film's ever-more-incoherent spaces as a kind of performer, delivering one-liners.'[7]

Steve Seidman and Frank Krutnik have argued that comedians like Harpo Marx and Charlie Chaplin are 'tricksters' or 'shape-shifters', capable of transforming themselves into inanimate objects and of adopting the traits of others.[8] Krutnik writes that a comedian also functions not as a 'localised' character but as a performer who is

> marked within the text as having a privileged status compared to other characters/actors: he is less functionally integrated and has a relatively disruptive function in relation to the fictional world and its codes of behaviour and action.[9]

Freddy is the comic who can move freely from one place to another. Residing in a world constructed through dreams, he can literally emerge in the environment of his choice: the beach of an exotic island in *Nightmare 4* or, in *Nightmare 5*, an asylum for the insane, which was the venue for both his mother's rape and his conception. With an established identity, Freddy's deviation from the fiction is easily accepted. When he appears as the new cook, complete with chef's hat, preparing to serve food to a dieting girl in *Nightmare 5*, we are at first unaware that the cook is in fact Freddy. It is only when we are able to see his face that his attire is rendered comically false. His impersonation of the chef is a perversely ironic comment on the status of the dieting girl.

Like the comedian, Freddy also functions disruptively in relation to the fictional world, by manipulating, destroying or even completely altering its structure. In being, however, a dream 'master', capable of recreating the fictional world in his own image, Freddy's status here is much stronger than that of other comedians. He is clearly able to disrupt the fictional world in a manner that other comedians cannot. Part of the comedian's disruptive function is a refusal to act 'straight' against the acting of the other characters in the film. In the *Nightmare* series no one other than Freddy appears to act out of character; everyone else consistently delivers both stable and 'sincere' performances. None of the films' characters can accept or perceive Freddy's humour. He is, as Kim Newman writes, a 'walking joke who kills his victims with a James-Bondish wisecrack'.[10] A notable example occurs in *Nightmare 4*, where

Freddy appears as a surgeon in the operating theatre in which Dan is lying. 'Krueger!' Dan exclaims, realising the surgeon's identity. 'Well it ain't Dr Seuss!' Freddy replies.

Freddy as a comedian does not perform for the appreciation of the characters within the films. Instead, he entertains and 'acknowledges' the subject watching the performance. Intervening between the overt fiction and the spectator, a space is established that is closer to the space of a theatre audience than that of a film audience. Umberto Eco noted that Walt Disney, in building Disneyland, achieved his personal dream of breaking down the wall of the second dimension and creating not a movie but total theatre.[11] It is this dream that is shared by the *Nightmare* films.

In an attempt to realise this vision, *Nightmare 6* presents a sequence in 3-D, which endeavours to efface the space that separates the viewer from the screen. This sequence occurs in the last fifteen minutes of the film, when Freddy eventually dies. Viewers were provided with special glasses through which at the appropriate time they could gain access to the space behind the screen. In the film, Doc hands a pair of 3-D glasses to Maggie, informing her that they have to be worn in order to defeat Freddy. Maggie puts on her glasses which dissolve into her face; this is the cue for the spectators to put on their own glasses. The film communicates directly here with the viewers, telling them what action they should take in order to continue a relation with the film's presentation. Failure to wear the glasses prevents spectators from being able to convert their space into an extension of the screen space. Not to wear the glasses would also imply a failure to defeat Freddy. For he is defeated not just by the characters on screen but also by the viewers who comply with the film's command and wear the glasses.

This attempt to efface the division between illusion and reality is continually explored throughout the *Nightmare* series. In *Nightmare 6* a boy who is interested in playing computer games is seduced by a psychedelic light show and is literally drawn into the television from which it is being emitted. Inside the television, he becomes a figure in a computer game, which Freddy is playing and controlling. Similarly, in *Nightmare 4* Alice is literally drawn into the space of the film she is watching. At the screening of a film, *Lost Burning Youth*, the black and white image suddenly transforms into an image of the cafeteria in which Alice works. In the film, a strong gale blows outside the cafeteria at the same time as a strong gale blows through the cinema auditorium. Finally, unable to hold herself down, Alice is sucked into the film. The audience in the theatre, unaffected by the gale, stands up and applauds. Now inside the screen, Alice observes the audience through the windows of the cafeteria that she had been viewing from her seat in the auditorium.

Unlike the previous films in the series, the seventh, *Wes Craven's New Nightmare*, is more concerned with narrative than spectacle, and has the most sustained interest in dissolving illusion and reality. The characters in this film, who are the film-makers involved in the production of the *Nightmare* series, are being destroyed by the Freddy that they have created. Freddy has been able to emerge from the fictional space of cinema into the 'real' space of the diegesis, the supposed reality of the film-makers, in which the crew and actors of the series play themselves: Wes Craven appears as Wes Craven the director, Heather Langenkamp appears as Langenkamp the actress, and Robert Englund is himself, the actor who has played Freddy in the films.

Generally speaking, the *Nightmare* films, acutely aware of their relationship with the audience, offer increasingly provocative images and situations. They attempt to establish a surface that will seduce the subject into the space of illusion, in which Freddy Krueger is the foregrounded image and principal attraction.

An example of this is the merchandising of products associated with the films. One of the more extraordinary of these products was a lifesize replica of Freddy Krueger's glove. This was marketed as a children's toy and was available from department stores and toy shops. The American advertising for the glove declared in large letters that 'You Too Can Become the Bastard Son of a Thousand Maniacs', while in slightly smaller letters around an image of the glove were placed the statements 'Soft Plastic Blades' and 'It's Play Safe!', under which was written 'Caution: do not use the glove in any violent manner'. It is remarkable that the weapon used by a child killer in a series of violent horror films should be marketed as a plaything for children. What is produced here is a simulacrum of the glove used by Freddy in the films, with the metal razor blades replaced by plastic copies. The disturbing reality of this is contextualised by Sheila Johnston, commenting on an event that took place in Hadonville, New Jersey on 31 October 1988:

> A bright sunny morning for the children's Halloween parade. Here among the usual ghoulies, ghosties and long-leggedy beasties, were a good half dozen eight-year olds kitted out in approximations of the Freddy uniform – felt hats, red-and-green striped sweaters, variously-simulated third degree facial burns, and the famous razor-fingered glove, which they waved merrily at the proud moms clustered round the gate.[12]

It is here that an extremely ironic situation develops. For the parents in *Nightmare 1* had supposedly incinerated Freddy Krueger for molesting and killing their children. In our reality, however, in the space that exists outside the film, parents actively encourage the presence of Freddy Krueger within their society. Whereas Freddy was destroyed for molesting children in the film, mothers are now content to see their children celebrating his character.

It would appear that Freddy had been released from the imaginary space of the film, 'possessing' the subject that exists outside the screen in which he had been contained. The child who dresses as Freddy has been seduced by the object. As with Jesse in *Nightmare 2*, the weaker identity of the subject is lost as it is replaced by the strong identity of Freddy. At the Halloween parade in Hadonfield, New Jersey, the children temporarily appeared to be more Freddy than child.

This seduction has been facilitated by the products associated with the *Nightmare* films. As Sheila Johnston notes, Alison Emilio of New Line announced in 1988 that they had been thinking of launching a range of 'Freddy-Chic' clothing.[13] This seemed never to materialise. However lifesize inflatable dolls and cardboard cut-outs were produced in order for the consumer to enjoy a closer union with Freddy. The object is here allowed to finally triumph over the subject, with the subject desiring either to resemble Freddy, or to acquire products that recreate parts of Freddy's identity.

A similar phenomenon occurs with respect to Freddy's fandom. According to Douglas Thompson in 1989, Freddy Krueger's fan club had more members than U2's.[14] In 1988 *Rolling Stone* observed that Freddy 'is perhaps as familiar a pop icon as any rock star of the day'. Indeed Freddy has had a record with his own dance called 'Do the Freddy' and has appeared occasionally as a presenter on the cable television rock station MTV.[15] He has also been 'honoured' by a number of hardcore porn films which imitate the form of the series: *A Nightmare on Porn Street* (1988), *Nightmare on Sex Street* (1991) and *Nightmare on Dyke Street* (1992).

Of further interest was Freddy's appearance in five editions of the *Daily Star* in September 1992. At a time when other newspapers carried headlines of conflict in the former Yugoslavia, on Monday 8 September the *Daily Star* carried a half-page image of Freddy Krueger on its front page. Issued with the paper were a pair of 3-D glasses, enabling the viewer to gain a closer relation with special images of Freddy presented on the paper's centre pages. Emphasising obvious aspects of Freddy, such as his glove, they were a relatively successful attempt at deconstructing the two-dimensional image, presenting Freddy as an object that could supposedly 'leap' out of the paper.

Despite this example, it is clear that Freddy is mainly marketed by appealing to young children. It is difficult, however, to understand fully how these children could be attracted to a figure who existed in films that were R-rated in America and given adult certificates in Britain.[16] One possibility is that children first accessed the films through the merchandising. The products would have assisted in Freddy's seduction of the subject and encouraged the child to develop an active interest in the films.

But the marketing of Freddy has gone much further than mere toys. Phone lines were established which children could dial and hear Freddy tell horrific stories. A children's story book of *Nightmare 1*, complete with graphic colour photographs, was published in the US, while bubblegum cards and watches with Freddy's face on the dial established him as an object that was omnipresent within the children's environment. Even an eighteen-inch talking Freddy doll was made available in 1989. The model, which in Britain was marketed by the respectable toy company Matchbox, was surprisingly for ages three and up. A well-crafted doll that bore a strong resemblance to Freddy, it had movable arms and legs and, if the cord on its back was pulled, could communicate a variety of messages: 'Pleasant dreams', 'Welcome to Elm Street', 'Watch out, Freddy's back', and the frightening suggestion 'Let's be friends'.

One of the board games made available, the US *A Nightmare on Elm Street* – The Freddy Game, produced by Cardinal in 1989 for ages eight and up, presented a situation in which the players move around Freddy's house, a cardboard construction in strong, bright colours.[17] Progress around the board is made by players selecting a counter which appears in the form of a character, who is clearly defined as suffering from a specific fear. If the player elects to be 'Grandpa' then the personal weakness is 'Empty Grave', while 'Cheerleader's fear is 'Freezing', 'Nice Guy's is 'Fire' and 'Mom's is 'Rodents'. The game includes a 'You Are Freddy!' card, which requires recipients to collect 'Razor Fingers' and permits them to destroy other players and even win the game. The instructions explain that 'In this game, one of the players will be "possessed" by Freddy Krueger ... but which one! – it could be you!'

A child's desire to become Freddy could be explained by Gary Heba's suggestion that there exists in horror films 'an ideological kinship of "otherness" between youth and the monster'.[18] Elders have regarded youths as threatening and disruptive as a result of their pre-adult interests and appearance. Young people are consequently able to identify with the monstrous as 'it, too, stands outside and apart from the members of dominant culture'.[19] Freddy, a monster with attitude and limitless power, makes subversion appear exciting.

While planning the launch of a *Nightmare* computer game, the films' producers conducted market research into whether children would prefer to be the Elm Street kids or Freddy Krueger. Most of those questioned replied that they would prefer to be Freddy. These children do not want to defeat Freddy but instead desire to protect and support his existence.

For them, it is the children in the films who need to be destroyed and not their killer.

Spin-offs from the *Nightmare* films were the number one selling merchandise of 1987, leading New Line's Alison Emilio to declare that Freddy was the 'Mickey Mouse of horror'.[20] Like Mickey Mouse, Freddy is instantly recognisable to children. As the Heather Langenkamp 'character' in *Nightmare 7* tells a nurse: 'Every kid knows who Freddy is. He is like Santa Claus.' The image of Freddy has been softened to such a degree that his appearance ceases to terrify some children. For instance, an eight-year-old girl in America dying of leukemia had a final wish to meet Freddy before she died. This was met with Robert Englund, the actor who plays Freddy, appearing in his 'costume' at her bedside. The young girl was not interested in meeting the actor who played Freddy, nor was she interested in meeting a more traditional children's idol. Instead, she, a dying girl, desired to meet Freddy Krueger himself, the killer of children. More important, it had to be the real Freddy, not a replica. When she met Robert Englund, in the original make-up and costume, it was as if Freddy had completely crossed over from the space of illusion into reality.

In the conclusion of *Nightmare 5* Alice's unborn son, Jacob, tells his mother, 'Mummy, meet my friend', with Freddy, in turn, telling Jacob, 'I'm your real friend, Jacob. Just like a daddy.' This is crucial, for Freddy arguably acts as a surrogate 'father' for the many children drawn to the films. He is there for the children as a close friend who is funny, powerful and fascinating and who will always be present to play with them. At the start of *Nightmare 3*, Alice arrives at Freddy's house. Sitting on the pavement outside is a little girl drawing. As Alice bends down towards the picture, the little girl turns around and declares 'Freddy's home!' Here, Freddy functions like a father who has returned home from work, a father whose arrival is eagerly awaited by the children. As the 'father', Freddy also always provides the children with good 'advice'. In *Nightmare 1*, he informs the frantic Nancy, who is racing through her school, that there is 'no running in the corridors'. While in *Nightmare 5*, he tells a boy obsessed with comics, 'Told you comic books were bad for you!', in *Nightmare 4*, he writes 'Learning is fun' on a girl's test paper. He becomes a form of counsel and guidance and a protector of the children. The counsellor, however, is perverted, for Freddy attacks the children who receive his advice.

The theme of paternity is present throughout the *Nightmare* series, with the later films in particular focusing on the paternal identity of Freddy. Jacob in *Nightmare 5* and Dylan in *Nightmare 7* are fatherless children. Both lost their fathers in road accidents caused by Freddy, which left him *in loco parentis*. In his 'stepfather' role, Freddy exploits his union with the child in order to gain entry to the 'real' world. The child is captivated by Freddy and encouraged to share in his power and knowledge. Jacob in *Nightmare 5* tells Freddy: 'Lets go! I want to learn from you', while Dylan, in *Nightmare 7*, appears in Langenkamp's dream wearing Freddy's glove. Similarly, in *Nightmare 6*, Spencer, who is trapped in a computer game, has to combat a computer figure of a father. As the figure repeats the line 'Be like me!', Freddy, who controls the game, declares, 'Father knows best!' In the film's conclusion, Maggie discovers that she is Freddy's daughter. Enticing her with the offer of unlimited power, Freddy invites her to try on his glove. It is an invitation that has been willingly accepted by children in our own reality. They have allowed themselves to be 'possessed', not only by Freddy but by consumerism itself.

Notes

1. *A Nightmare on Elm Street* figure from *Variety* MIFED issue (15 October 1990), p. M140, all other figures from *Variety* Cannes film market issue (10 May 1993), pp. C76, C86.
2. See the following books by Jean Baudrillard for a discussion of the object, the subject and seduction: *The Ecstasy of Communication* (New York: Semiotext(e), 1988), *Fatal Strategies* (London: Pluto, 1990) and *Revenge of the Crystal* (London: Pluto, 1990). In *Fatal Strategies*, Baudrillard writes:

> In our philosophy of desire, the subject retains an absolute privilege, since it is the subject that desires. But everything is inverted if one passes on to the thought of seduction. There, it's no longer the subject

which desires, it's the object which seduces. Everything comes from the object and everything returns to it, just as everything started with seduction, not with desire. The immemorial privilege of the subject is overthrown. For the subject is fragile and can only desire, whereas the object gets on very well even when desire is absent; the object seduces through the absence of desire; it plays on the other with the effect of desire, provoking or annuling it, exalting and deceiving it. (pp. 111–12)

3. Sheila Johnston, 'Clawing in the cash', *Independent*, 10 November 1988, p. 19.
4. Henry Jenkins, 'Killing time on Elm Street: Freddy Krueger and the post-classical horror film', unpublished conference paper, University of East Anglia (1991), p. 6.
5. Jeffrey Sconce, 'Spectacles of death: identification, reflexivity, and contemporary horror', in Jim Collins, Hilary Radner and Ava Preacher Collins (eds), *Film Theory Goes to the Movies* (London: Routledge, 1993), pp. 113–14.
6. David Edelstein, 'Drilling for fresh nerves', *Village Voice* 20 November 1984, p. 58.
7. Jenkins, 'Killing time', p. 7.
8. Steve Seidman, *Comedian Comedy: A Tradition in Hollywood Film* (UMI Research Press, 1981) *passim*; Frank Krutnik, 'The clown-prints of comedy', *Screen* 25, 4–5 (July–October 1984), pp. 50–9.
9. Krutnik, 'The clown-prints of comedy', p. 51.
10. Kim Newman, '*A Nightmare on Elm Street 4: The Dream Master*', *Monthly Film Bulletin* 664 (May 1989), p. 146.
11. Umberto Eco, *Travels in Hyperreality* (London: Picador, 1987), p. 45.
12. Johnston, 'Clawing in the cash', p. 19.
13. Ibid.
14. Douglas Thompson, 'Freddy – the man of your dreams', *You* magazine, *Mail on Sunday*, 2 April 1989, p. 28.
15. 'Fab Freddy', *Rolling Stone*, 6 October 1988, p. 92.
16. *Nightmares 1–6* received an 18 certificate (film suitable only for persons of 18 years and over) for their theatrical release in the UK; *Nightmare 7* received a 15 certificate (film suitable only for persons of 15 years and over). *Nightmares*

1–7 received an 18 classification for their release on video cassette in the UK. In one of the many self-reflexive moments in *Nightmare 7*, a nurse severely criticises Heather Langenkamp for supposedly allowing her young son to watch the *Nightmare* films.

17. Another game was the US *A Nightmare on Elm Street – The Game*, produced by Victory Games in 1987, for ages 8 to adult. The game begins in the 'Nightmare Zone'; other areas are 'The House' and 'Boiler Room'. The instructions state that 'You are asleep, adrift in the land where Freddy roams, and you have to wake up ... you try to move your pawn through a maze to the Awake side of the board ... if you are crafty enough, you can use Freddy's moves to attack other players who are getting too far ahead of you.'

18. Gary Heba, 'Everyday nightmares: the rhetoric of social horror in the *Nightmare on Elm Street* series', *Journal of Popular Film and Television* 23, 3 (Fall 1995), p. 108.

19. Ibid.

20. Johnston, 'Clawing in the cash', p. 19.

I would like to thank Sarah Davy, Peter Kramer and Paul Danbury for their invaluable comments and suggestions.

8

Cinematic Novels and 'Literary' Films: *The Shining* in the Context of the Modern Horror Film

Steve Cramer

The many and varied readings of Stanley Kubrick's *The Shining* (1980) by the critical industry have tended to concentrate on the father–son relationship portrayed in the film. From William Paul's reading, which he titles 'The revenge of Oedipus' to other psychoanalytic readings such as Dickstein's 'The aesthetics of fright', the central metaphor for most critics is the disruption of forms of male bonding.[1] Other critics, such as Mario Falsetto, have concentrated upon individual male characters. Falsetto cites Jack as central to the film through the individual point-of-view Steadicam shots which frequently represent him.[2] My intention is not to refute such views entirely, but to reassess them from the perspective of that specific subgenre of the horror film, the haunted house film. It is by contrasting the genre-fixated novel of Stephen King with the metageneric techniques of Kubrick that we arrive at the centrality of Wendy to the film. Her character has been largely dismissed by critics as a necessary function. Like Isabel in Wordsworth's 'Michael', she is represented as the necessary blood link between father and son, an objectified entity whose existence preserves the wholeness of the nuclear family. King draws upon what he has identified in his study of horror in film and fiction, *Danse Macabre*, as the essential conservatism of the form, and in his constant citation of cinematic precedent in the novel he reaffirms this ideology.[3]

It is in the central female character that we see King's preference for particular generic conventions in the haunted house movie. It is surprising that so little attention has been paid by critics to the figure of Wendy Torrance in *The Shining*.

In King's novel she reprises a succession of female central characters in the haunted house film by relinquishing her nurturing role in favour of indulging her sexuality.[4] In the critical moment of the novel, after Danny's assault by the woman in room 217, Wendy proposes leaving the Overlook by means of the snowmobile. However, she is distracted by Jack's sexual advances, eventually deferring her journey until the next day, by which time Jack, by now thoroughly possessed by the hotel, has rendered the snowmobile inoperable. King loads this episode with heavy-handed moral symbolism. While Danny is in the room asleep, watched over by his mother, the narration's self-consciously male gaze focuses exclusively on Wendy's breasts, as Jack first fondles, then sucks them. The disembodied agent of nurture is sexualised and the passage ends with Wendy's allusion to T.S. Eliot's *The Waste Land*:

> She had taken off her shirt and lay on the bed, her belly flat, her breasts aimed perkily at the ceiling. She was playing with them lazily, flicking at the nipples. 'Hurry up, gentlemen', she said softly, 'time'. (p. 247)

The additional intertextual reference, conjuring up the conversation on abortion in 'A Game of Chess' further delineates Wendy's abnegation of her mothering role.

For all the use of learned intertextuality implied by King's allusion to Eliot, this apportioning of blame for the later events of the novel to Wendy is more to do with movies than books. Aside from the odd one-off allusion such as the one quoted above, it is the tradition of Gothic fiction to which King claims to pay homage in *The Shining*. But as Bunnell points out in her assessment of the Gothic tradition, it is by resisting the sexual advances of male characters in isolated houses on Romantic landscapes that female characters survive in such early Gothic novels as Radcliffe's *The Mysteries of Udolpho* (1794).[5]

King's Wendy Torrance falls more in line with the succession of sexualised females in the haunted house film since 1960. In Jack Clayton's *The Innocents* (1961) – an adaptation of Henry James' *The Turn of the Screw* (1898) – Deborah Kerr's sexually frustrated governess becomes erotically obsessed with her predecessor's affair with the late Peter Quint, thereby bringing about the psychological destruction of the girl and death of the boy in her care. Similarly, in John Hough's *The Legend of Hell House* (1973), Florence Tanner (Pamela Franklin), the medium employed to uncover the secret of the haunted Nolasco house, assumes a mothering role to the ghost of the adolescent son of the equally ghostly Hell House patriarch, but is finally seduced by him, and turns instantly from an evangelistic Christian spinster to a human succubus, helping to release the evil spirits which haunt Hell House. In Robert Wise's *The Haunting* (1963) Eleanor Lance finds herself reappraising her role in the death of her mother, whose final calls from her death-bed she had ignored, just as the late owner of Hill House, a slatternly housekeeper, had ignored the calls for assistance of her elderly employer, being preoccupied with the advances of an unnamed young man.

The source of real horror in the haunted house film, then, is untrammelled female sexuality. In contrast to Shelley Duvall's self-consciously plain, housewifely Wendy, complete with serviceable terry-towelling bathrobe, smock and overalls, King's Wendy is, significantly, first described 65 pages into the novel, on her arrival at the Overlook:

[Ullman] shook hands with Jack and nodded coolly at Wendy, perhaps noticing the way heads turned when she came through into the lobby, her golden hair spilling across the shoulders of her simple navy dress. The hem of her dress stopped a modest two inches above the knee, but you didn't have to see more to know that they were good legs. (p. 65)

This combination of demureness and latent sexuality alerts the reader to Wendy's impending fall, encoding the character within a prefabricated archetype, that of the woman obedient to patriarchal imperative, but tainted with a mature sexuality. She is liable to disrupt the established order by libidinal outbursts such as those manifested by the equally demure figures of Julie Harris, Pamela Franklin, Gayle Hunnicutt and Deborah Kerr in the earlier cinematic ghost stories. Wendy's responsibility for the later events of the novel, rather than

Jack's, is emphasised by the repeated assurance that the character who terrifies his family at the end of the novel is not Jack, but simply his body, animated by the various spirits of the hotel.

In Kubrick's film, by contrast, it is Jack who is sexualised by ghostly presences. Whereas in the novel Jack's investigation of Room 217 leads only to the smell of soap, and the impression that he is pursued out of the room by an invisible presence, Kubrick's version turns Jack Torrance into Jack the Lad. As Mario Falsetto points out, Jack's supreme self-reflexivity provides Kubrick with endless opportunities for subjective tracking-shots.[6] Few are more important than the one in which Jack's hand is seen to push open the bathroom door of Room 217, and we see, from Jack's point of view, the emergence of the room's ghostly presence. Falsetto's claim for the objective presence of the woman who emerges from the bath, however, is belied by the succession of close-up reaction shots of Jack as his expression turns from fear to leering lasciviousness. The impassiveness of the woman in the bath seems similarly geared towards designating male wish-fulfilment. When Jack walks over to her after she has emerged from the bath and disported herself in half-profile under the bathroom light, as if to maximise the advantage for the male gaze, he stares at her for some time, and in a projection of male potency against female passivity, it is she who finally puts her arms around his neck. Jack then experiences full frontal, if you will, Kristeva's abjection. In other words, the authoritarian father figure encounters, through his subjectivised woman, the abjection of his own body. In a sense, Jack represents three aspects of Kristeva's textual disseminations, beginning the scene as the father figure of the Symbolic realm (phallocentric, authoritarian, repressed), then in his sexual fantasy touching upon the Semiotic (pre-Oedipal, transgressive), even given that his shock responses to the woman ultimately return him to the Symbolic. Finally, the living corpse, covered as it is in sores and putrefaction, returns Jack to his corporealness, to the fact of his declining body. The corpse as a physical presence represents both the taboo of death, and as a woman, of sexual difference.[7] Significantly it is the bathroom mirror which provides Jack with the information that his own physical decrepitude (reflected before by the contrasting appearance of Jack's fantasy woman and his own dishevelment) is forever approaching. The fact that the animated corpse of the old woman has come from Jack's own projections of otherness makes the point even more directly that Jack's notion of beauty represents a sustained deferral of his subliminal awareness of abjection. Jack is pursued from the room by the mocking and deflating laughter of the old woman, bathetically reducing the earlier fantasy of male potency, just as the point of view and reverse angle shots of the pictures of naked women with afros on Halloran's wall mock Halloran's total baldness in the scene which prefaces this.[8]

The majority of critics of the film have concentrated on the over-the-top performance of Jack Nicholson as being central to the film's parodic relationship to its generic paradigm. But this is to underrate Shelley Duvall's character, whose centrality to the film's metageneric processes is illustrated by Jack's first comment on Wendy's character. Before the audience sees her it is told that she is 'a confirmed ghost story and horror film addict'. The significance of this is borne out by Wendy's appearance with Danny in the following scene, as she watches a *Road Runner* cartoon, the first prefiguring of the film's later shifting of formal apparatus from horror film to savage farce. It is she, too, who provides so much of the physical action which traduces the film's genre choice. Her run up the stairs to discover two men, one dressed as a dog, engaged in oral sex in an upper bedroom represents a burlesque of the conventional helpless female of the horror film, a thirteenth stroke of the clock worthier of Joe Orton than Richard Matheson or Shirley Jackson. Her rolling eyes and deft use of a lanky body made her the obvious casting choice for Olive Oyl in *Popeye* (1980). It is also Wendy who uncovers the final joke about the Colorado Lounge in the longer version of the film. While Jack's two visits to the hotel bar reveal the same group of bland and emotionless faces, another subjectified transference of desire, this time for power and, no less important, alcohol, Wendy races into the bar to find a great mass of grinning, cobweb-covered skeletons. Once again, Wendy is the agent of shifting narratives, debunking the earlier ghostly apparitions of Jack's mind by reformulating them into figures from that long-dead genre, the old dark house movie. Her reaction shot is worthy of the horror parody *The Cat and the Canary* (1978), and the hammy joke implied by this trope can only be seen as comical.

In a sense, the movement of the film into burlesque describes a resistance to the urge for loving imitation, perhaps most notably manifested in Herzog's *Nosferatu the Vampyre* in 1979, in which Isobel Adjani's sylph-like victim status and dangerous sexual responsiveness to Klaus Kinski's vampire maintains uncritically a commodified view of the woman in the horror film which had stood for over half a century.

Commodity is a central value of the haunted house film. The 'you get what you pay for' consumerist shibboleth can be easily attached to such films as *Burnt Offerings* (1976) and *The Amityville Horror* (1979), illustrating that a low-cost summer rent in the former case and an extremely modest buying price in the latter can have destructive results. James Brolin's patriarch, George Lutz, in *Amityville* characterises the economic anxiety attendant upon the horror film male, also exemplified by Luke in *The Haunting*, whose frightening experiences begin after he has come to Hill House to gauge its property value. George Lutz's business runs down after his arrival at Amityville, because his increasing obsession with the house causes him to neglect his small company. Academic work is also ill-fated in the haunted house film. Dr Marquis' paper is not written at Hill House, and he displays a general incompetence about the geography of the house and interpretation of its supernatural events which seems to indicate that it never will be. Dr Barret fares still worse at Hell House. He is killed after attempting to use his anti-ghost machine, joining Florence Tanner, who has met the wrath of God reserved for loose women, crushed under a gigantic crucifix. All of this is indicative of the general anti-intellectualism of the postmodern interpretation of Gothic in the cinema and King's novel, where rational discourse is overwhelmed by pre-rational forces.

Work is at the centre of Kubrick's film. The job at the hotel represents a last chance for Jack in both film and book. A reformed alcoholic, Jack is subject to possible unemployment and must show dedication to his job and reintegrate into family life. The novel documents his failure to do so, while the book ironises the underlying ideology of consumerised conformity by positing the idea that Jack has successfully reformed his attitude to work and family life, and has gone mad in the process. In his final moments he resorts to the suburban husband's greeting, 'Wendy, I'm home!' as he axes down the door of the family apartment. Similarly, as he breaks through the bathroom door, Wendy and Danny's last rampart of protection, he alludes to the ultimate American family show, with 'Here's Johnny!' These words are, of course, not Johnny Carson's but Ed McMahon's, the eternal employee and assistant to Johnny, and the endless subject of 'What do I pay you for' jokes. The joke, which both Kubrick and Nicholson claimed to have improvised on set, represents an acknowledgement and acceptance of Jack's role as caretaker rather than novelist. Increasingly in the film, the hotel represents a stability of employment which is not represented elsewhere in an America on the verge of electing Ronald Reagan President. When on the grand staircase of the hotel he confronts Wendy about whether they should leave the Overlook (a scene which effectively supplants King's seduction scene) he argues that he will finish up shovelling snow out of driveways, and cites his 'obligation to my employers' as a reason to stay. He rounds off with the question: 'Have you any idea what a moral and ethical principle is?'

The inclusion of the moral and the ethical within the same question leads us to Fredric Jameson's reading of *The Shining*, which points out that a conventional haunted house narrative is short-circuited by the fact that the house in question is not a private space, but a hotel, making an uncontestable claim to be a public space.[9] This renders King's complaint that Kubrick had turned his novel with its central concern with the supernatural into what he called 'a domestic tragedy' redundant: the film's superficial narrative structure concerns itself with the domestic, but the personal is rendered political by its locale. The focal point of the genre, Jameson tells us, is history, since the haunted house represents a continual reminder of the past. Astutely, he also points out that whereas the novel locates its ghosts in no specific historical moment since the building of the hotel, the film turns all of its ghosts into figures from the 1920s:

The twenties were the last moment in which a genuine American leisure class led an aggressive and ostentatious existence, in which an American ruling-class projected a class-conscious and unapologetic image of itself, and enjoyed its privileges without guilt, openly and armed with its emblems of top-hat and champagne glass, on the social stage in full view of the other classes.[10]

Jameson's reading finds the film 'disturbing for both Left and Right alike', since the image of the twenties represents not only an historicising allegory for the present day, but also in Jack's literary aspirations a repressed desire to return to older forms of rigid hierarchy.

But it is surely the figure of Jack which the film most condemns for his aspirational reintegration, individuating him as insane in his final embrace of the work ethic and 'family values'. This is borne out particularly by the opposite direction in which the novel moves. Stephen King's defence of his work after his condemnation by the *Village Voice* illustrates the right-wing ideology which informs his novel:

There's a political element in that *Voice* attack. You see, I view the world with what is essentially an old-fashioned frontier vision. I believe that people can master their own destiny and can confront and overcome tremendous odds. I'm convinced that there exist absolute values of good and evil warring for supremacy in this universe – which is, of course, a basic religious viewpoint. And – what damns me even more in the eyes of the 'enlightened' cognoscenti – I also believe that traditional values of family, fidelity, and personal honour have not at all drowned in the trendy California hot-tub of the 'me' generation. That puts me at odds with what is essentially an urban and liberal sensibility that equates all change with progress, and wants to destroy all conventions in literature as well as society.[11]

What condemns Jack in King's novel is not integration but failure to integrate into this right-wing vision of society. Jack is here portrayed as a left-wing Democrat, unlike King, a right-wing Democrat who appears to have no objection to

Republican economic policies, condemning welfare spending in one of his interviews but opposing the banning of his books, possibly for sound economic reasons. Jack hears from Ullman, the hotel's manager, that four American presidents – Harding, Roosevelt, Kennedy and Nixon – have stayed at the Overlook, and dislikes the idea of Harding and Nixon having resided there. Later, his psychological breakdown is prefigured by an elaborate conspiracy theory which he constructs while repairing the roof of the hotel. He comes to believe that his sacking from his former job as a college teacher for beating up a particularly privileged student was an act of savage retribution by a comfortable cabal of upper-class Americans. Jack at first denies, then much later admits to himself, that he removed the boy from the college debating team on the pure and simple grounds of Jack's class resentment. Similarly, he resents and eventually attacks by telephone Al Shockley, a benevolent millionaire who, like a Dickensian *deus ex machina*, has arrived to save Jack from unemployment in the nick of time, providing him with his job at the Overlook. Shockley too becomes a part of the conspiracy, and we begin to see that Jack, in King's view, represents that bogey of the New Right, a 'loser' who is motivated not by 'the frontier spirit' or the desire 'to confront and overcome tremendous odds', but by the politics of envy, the desire to blame his own shortcomings on his society.

The two characters above do not come into the film at all, indicating Kubrick's desire to subvert King's ideological prejudices, but it is perhaps Mr Ullman, little more than a narrative function in Kubrick's film, who most bears out King's view of the social structure. The hotel manager, in King's version, is an autocratic boss who makes it clear to Jack from the outset that he does not want to employ him but has been forced to do so by Al Shockley. King portrays Ullman as homosexual, putting him beyond the bounds of family values. His unpleasantness is counterbalanced, though, by Mr Shockley, who demonstrates a reassuring knowledge by those in authority of what is best for such people as hotel caretakers. Ullman makes for King the point which is endlessly reiterated in the American mainstream film, that the system itself is not in fact faulty, but that certain maladjusted individuals can make it seem so.

Whereas it is the world of work which condemns Jack in Kubrick's film, it is his fecklessness and ultimate lack of dedication which destroys him in King's novel. Instead of attending to the hotel's ancient boiler in the basement, Jack becomes fascinated by the record of press clippings and receipts contained by the gigantic room, neglecting work for further data which might contribute to an ingenious narrative of corruption in the upper classes, the construction of which amounts ultimately to nothing in the novel. It is by his neglect of his work that Jack ultimately perishes, for in the finale of the novel the other *deus ex machina*, Halloran, does not subvert audience expectations as he does in the film, where he arrives at the Overlook to be immediately killed, but instead facilitates the escape of Wendy and Danny as Jack is blown up by the symbol of his neglect of the work ethic. The hotel goes with him, obligingly providing a satisfying narrative closure for its genre-fixated audience. The cinema comes in here too, the fiery destruction of the evil place bringing to its audience a reminder of *The Fall of the House of Usher*, not Poe's version, to which King has made endless ham-fisted intertextual references, but Corman's 1960 film adaptation. A great cloud forms itself into a demonic shape above the wreck of the hotel, also bringing in cinema traditions by citing quite clearly Roy Ward Baker's *Quatermass and the Pit* (1967). By contrast, the Jack Torrance of the film dies in the maze, 'a maze of the mind' as William Paul puts it.[12] Paul's interpretation runs along the lines that the maze (which does not exist in the novel, there being instead a topiary, whose animal sculptures come to life, a trope which King himself later felt to be ineffective) is largely there to facilitate our understanding of Danny and the learning process which the trope represents for him. But it might also be metaphorised as the maze of Jack's mind, of his endless, solipsistic and self-reflexive bourgeois individualist ethos. Significantly it is the film's career-oriented Jack who dies in a place of recreation rather than the neglected place of work of the novel. 'All work and no play makes Jack a dull boy' indeed.

It is with this central text of the film that we might return to Wendy, for it is by her disseminations of text, Jack's 'novel', quoted above, and the other male character Danny's 'redrum', that she illustrates her central metanarrative function. By her textual and subtextual literacy, she provides redemption for herself and her son at two critical moments of the film, where the difference between life and death is contingent upon the understanding of semiotic structures.

Notes

1. William Paul, *Laughing Screaming: Modern Hollywood Horror and Comedy* (New York: Columbia University Press, 1994), pp. 337–50; Morris Dickstein, 'The aesthetics of fright', in Barry Keith Grant (ed.), *Planks of Reason: Essays on the Horror Film* (London: Scarecrow Press, 1984), pp. 65–78.
2. Mario Falsetto, *Stanley Kubrick: A Narrative and Stylistic Analysis* (London: Praeger, 1994), pp. 164–73.
3. Stephen King, *Danse Macabre* (London: NEL, 1982).
4. Stephen King, *The Shining* (London: NEL, 1977). All page references in my text cite this edition.
5. Charlene Bunnell, 'The gothic: a literary genre's translation to film', in Grant, *Planks of Reason*, pp. 79–100.
6. Falsetto, *Stanley Kubrick*, pp. 131–40.
7. Julia Kristeva, *Powers of Horror: An Essay on Abjection* (New York: Columbia University Press, 1982).
8. The reader might observe the striking resemblance between this sequence and the dream episode in Mary Shelley's *Frankenstein* (1818), in which Victor embraces Elizabeth, then finds her turning into the animated corpse of his dead mother. Kubrick's Gothic 'literacy' seems in this way to locate his text through precedents older than that of King. Genre 'purity' is carefully located before it is subverted.
9. Fredric Jameson, *Signatures of the Visible* (New York: Routledge, 1992), p. 95.
10. Ibid.
11. George Beahm (ed.), *The Stephen King Companion* (London: Macdonald, 1989), p. 43.
12. Paul, *Laughing Screaming*, pp. 338–9.

9

'It's Always 1895': Sherlock Holmes in Cyberspace

Roberta Pearson

'Make a long arm Watson, and see what V has to say'.
I leaned back and took down the great index volume
to which [Holmes] referred. Holmes' ... eyes moved slowly
and lovingly over the record of old cases, mixed with the
accumulated information of a lifetime.
'Voyage of the *Gloria Scott* ... Victor Lynch, the forger.
Venomous lizard or gila ... Vittoria, the circus belle.
Vanderbilt and the Yeggman. Vipers. Vigor, the
Hammersmith wonder. Hullo! Hullo! Good old index. You
can't beat it. Vampirism in Hungary'.[1]

Although Holmes exclaimed in delight at finding an entry on
vampires, one wonders how the great detective ever managed
to locate anything in the commonplace books that he so
assiduously constructed and cross-indexed. A cataloguing
method that included both the voyage of the *Gloria Scott* and
Victor Lynch under the letter V does not seem conducive to
the quick retrieval of information. In fact, despite Holmes' nod
to linearity through alphabetisation, the grouping seems a
potentially hypertextual one. Were Holmes still in practice
today, one warrants that a high-powered PC, a collection of
CD-ROMs and a modem would beat the good old index hands
down. Such electronic marvels are, of course, the descendants
and latter-day equivalents of the commonplace books – all
devices intended for the storage, accessing and processing of
knowledge. Modern policemen, or, for that matter, modern
fictional crimefighters, with their huge databases and
connections to the World Wide Web, still engage in the same
search for relevant data as their nineteenth-century predecessor,

143

but can now trade information with colleagues round the world.

Sherlock Holmes fans, known as Sherlockians in the US and Holmesians in Britain, also engage in a detective process, priding themselves on emulating the Master's methods, as they seek to solve textual and other riddles: where was Watson's war wound; why did Holmes never marry; who first played Holmes on the stage? Once primarily dependent on cumbersome reference volumes that equalled the commonplace books in size and inclusiveness, but were much more insistently linear in their organisation, Sherlockians now also use computers in their search for and trading of information on the life and times of the great detective and the man who created him, Sir Arthur Conan Doyle. If one views computers as the logical extension of Holmes' own practices and habits of mind, the use of the latest twentieth-century technology by a readership that defines itself through affinity with a nineteenth-century popular hero appears reasonable. But, from another perspective, it seems rather puzzling that Sherlockians, who proudly proclaim that 'It's always 1895', can wholeheartedly embrace a technology that is so emphatically Windows 95.

This chapter explores that paradox, focusing on the Sherlockian bulletin board service, the Hounds of the Internet, or Hounds-L. I will suggest that a tension exists between the mythic and the historic in the Hounds' discussions of Victorian history in relation to the Holmesian canon. In addition, I will speculate that the Hounds' experience of history may be qualitatively transformed by their participation in computer mediated communication (CMC), as the historical, mediated through the latest technology, becomes a constant factor in their everyday lives.[2] The argument constructs itself at the intersection of several ongoing scholarly inquiries concerning fandom, computer mediated communication and the mediated representation of history. It is also part of a larger project concerning the diachronic and synchronic ideological appropriation of popular heroes. Before returning to the central topic of the Hounds and history, then, permit me to digress somewhat in order to provide what scriptwriters refer to as 'backstory'.

This chapter is part of a larger project on popular heroes and their ideological appropriations, following work by Bennett and Woollacott on James Bond and by Pearson and Uricchio on Batman.[3] Both Bond and Batman owe their longevity partially to their mutability; the characters are shifting signifiers relatively easily reconfigured to suit different ideological formations. Holmes shares this mutability. During the late nineteenth and early twentieth centuries, Sherlock Holmes apotheosised the scientific rationalism on which the period predicated its notions of progressive history as well as its domination over 'lesser breeds without the law'. Since his first appearance in the pages of the 1887 *Beeton's Christmas Annual*, Holmes has been appropriated for various ideological projects: a 1940s Holmes worked for the Allies; a 1970s Holmes uncovered a monstrous royal conspiracy in the film *Murder by Decree* (1979); and a 1980s Holmes featured in a series of heritage television programmes produced by Granada.

Conformity to broad ideological trajectories, however, precludes neither contradictions within single texts nor contradictory representations across multiple texts produced at the same time. In the original fifty-six short stories and four short novels that constitute what Sherlockians refer to as 'the canon' or 'the sacred writings', Holmes upholds bourgeois order but is himself a bohemian, drug-taking and eccentric bachelor without much tolerance for social conventions or for the less useful members of the upper classes, Her Majesty's Government and the Metropolitan Police. Among many examples of roughly contemporaneous yet contradictory portrayals, the playful nostalgia of Billy Wilder's *The Private Life of Sherlock Holmes* (1970) balanced the dark cynicism of the 1979 *Murder by Decree*.

Contradictions such as those seen in these two texts will remain a general condition of Holmes texts, but computers will certainly inevitably affect both access to historical representations and the ideological appropriations of popular heroes. This is not to take a technologically determinist position, for, of course, information technologies are both produced by and productive of the widespread social/cultural forces of modernity and postmodernity. But rejecting technological determinism does not preclude the intuitive recognition that computer mediated communications may entail effects that remain hard to articulate within available language structures. Deborah Lupton has written a very provocative article about computer use and the sense of self that touches on this issue:

> Users invest certain aspects of themselves and their cultures when 'making sense' of their computers and their use of computers may be viewed as contributing to individuals' images and experiences of their selves and their bodies. Our interactions with PCs inscribe our bodies, so that, for example, pens start to feel awkward as writing instruments.[4]

Most of us would probably agree that learning to write with a word processor affected, if not our sense of self, at least our writing style, and, extrapolating from this, might be willing to speculate that CMC might produce similar, and perhaps, more far-reaching consequences. Yet many commentators, such as the guru of CMC, Harold Rheingold, take a curiously traditionalist perspective that extends even to the old metaphors they use to characterise the new technology. Rheingold claims that CMC has proven so attractive to so many because of

> the hunger for community that grows in the breasts of people around the world as more and more informal public spaces disappear from our real lives. I also suspect that those new media attract colonies of enthusiasts because CMC enables people to do things with each other in new ways, and to do altogether new kinds of things – just as telegraphs, telephones and televisions did.[5]

Despite the technologically determinist assertion that CMC will produce new behaviour patterns, the title of Rheingold's book, *The Virtual Community: Homesteading on the Electronic Frontier*, harks back to behaviour patterns more than a century old; the ruggedly individualist 'pioneers' of CMC are seen as metaphorically building new communities in newly tamed regions of cyberspace. Here the members will establish electronic public spheres that will serve the same functions as the eighteenth-century coffee houses beloved of Jurgen Habermas.

Questions of community are central to many of the scholars studying the new medium. In fact there is at least one recently published book wholly devoted to the topic and students, from undergraduates to postgraduates, seem obsessed by the topic.[6] It matters not what subjects initially bring people together or what they subsequently discuss as long as they can be said to have formed a virtual community. This focus on community causes many scholars to seem more concerned with the form of CMC than with the content. We learn about the substitution of 'emoticons' for the facial expressions and gestures of f-t-f (face-to-face) communication or about free speech versus netiquette or about the conventions of community maintenance. But while we might know a great deal about how people talk on the Net we do not yet know much concerning what it is that they actually talk about or how the experience of this talk might differ from the experience of more conventional modes of interaction.

In this chapter I want to explore the proposition that computer mediated communication may change the nature of historical memory. Alison Landsberg speaks of 'prosthetic memories', by which she means:

> memories which do not come from a person's lived experience in any strict sense. These are implanted memories, and the unsettled boundaries between real and simulated ones are frequently accompanied by another disruption: of the human body, its flesh, its subjective autonomy, its difference from both animal and technological.[7]

The term 'prosthetic memory' is unfortunately as imprecise as it is intriguing. Landsberg initially derives the idea from the science fiction films *Total Recall* (1990) and *Johnny Mnemonic* (1995), whose heroes literally have foreign memories implanted in their brains, films which in turn derived their plots from science fiction writers such as Philip K. Dick and William Gibson. As Landsberg acknowledges, however, from a perspective which sees media consumption as divorced from 'real life' experience, the ubiquitous mass media threaten entirely to replace 'real' memories with 'prosthetic' memories. I would like to suggest that, as more and more people go on-line, computer mediated communication may also play a large role in the construction of 'prosthetic memories'. The interactive nature of the Internet, where it is possible to construct/link to homepages, subscribe/post to bulletin board services and lurk on/post to newsgroups, results in the same users simultaneously constructing 'prosthetic memories' *for* others while downloading 'prosthetic memories' constructed *by* others. In a metaphorical sense, then, Sherlockians in cyberspace may then be said both to produce and consume prosthetic memories of history, even though Internet communication does not result in the literal implantation of memories in their 'wetware'.

This chapter deals with differences between appropriations of Holmes in popular prosthetic memories constructed in computer mediated communication. I want to argue that members of one discursive community, the Hounds of the Internet, can produce very different appropriations of the same popular hero at the same historical moment. The appropriation shared by the majority of the Hounds seems congruent with the majority of representations of Holmes; a nostalgia for the Victorian past coupled with a conventional historiography of 'facts' and great men. The less prevalent, but perhaps more interesting, appropriation contests both nostalgia for the Victorian age and conventional notions of the historiographic.

One more digression for relevant backstory before proceeding to this argument. While media fandom has elicited an ever-growing body of literature[8] and while the Sherlock Holmes texts have been studied by semioticians and literary theorists,[9] Sherlock Holmes fans have remained blissfully untroubled by academics (until now, that is). A few words about Sherlockians are in order. The first official Sherlockians, those readers who successfully responded to a quiz in Christopher Morley's column in *The Saturday Review*, gathered at a New York City drinking establishment in 1934. There they formed the Baker Street Irregulars (BSI), the first and most famous of Sherlockian societies, named after the street urchins whom Holmes occasionally employed to assist him. Holmes fandom remains primarily an Anglo-American phenomenon, with more than a hundred of the so-called 'scion societies' in the US and several in Britain, including the premiere English organisation, the Sherlock Holmes Society of London. But Holmes societies flourish in what might seem unlikely venues; there are several in the Scandinavian countries and my Sherlockian informants tell me that there are close to 6000 Japanese Sherlockians.

While other fan clubs, certainly those devoted to Hollywood stars for example, may predate the BSI, the organisation and its subsequent scion societies around the US and around the world, may constitute the first truly bottom-up fandom. Although admittedly instigated by a column in an élite journal of the New York literary establishment and initially composed of members of that same establishment, Sherlockian fandom has never been hijacked by a media megaglomerate. Sherlockians participate in the mass commodification of their popular hero but on a sporadic basis as various corporations, large and small, see fit to market various Sherlockian commodities – books, films, games and so forth – Sherlockians, however, have never been subjected to the same media blitz as *Star Trek* or *Batman* fans.[10] Despite these distinctions between Sherlock Holmes fandom and media fandoms such as that surrounding *Star Trek*, Sherlockians engage in similar activities to other fans.[11] Members of scion societies meet on a regular basis to eat, drink, take quizzes, listen to talks, engage in theatrical presentations, sing, play games and, most importantly, escape into a world where all the inhabitants share a similar passion. Individual Sherlockians produce Sherlockian 'art' – ranging from paintings to hand-painted T-shirts – for their own pleasure or for sale.

But the activity that most concerns me here is Sherlockian writing, which takes three main forms. The founding members of the Baker Street Irregulars, together with English authors such as Ronald Knox and Dorothy Sayers, began the tradition of Sherlockian scholarship, at its best a parody of the academic tradition, employing the techniques of textual hermeneutics to clarify the contradictions and lacunae that stemmed from Conan Doyle's writing in the serial format. These 'writings on the writings' are based upon the premise that Holmes and Watson really lived and that Conan Doyle was merely the 'literary agent' who facilitated the publication of stories actually authored by Watson. Other Sherlockians have engaged in a more traditional auteurism, accepting Conan Doyle as the writer and explicating the stories by reference to his biography and other works. Both the whimsical and the serious writings draw upon the social/cultural context of Victorian Britain to elucidate textual conundrums, a tendency which seems even more pronounced in CMC than in print. For example, in a debate concerning Conan Doyle's knowledge of the proper forms of address for titled nobility, a member of the Hounds of the Internet, 'The Hon. Ronald Adair' wrote, 'I'm certainly not titled but I believe forms of address were very important in the Victorian era, not only among the British but those of British stock who were scattered around the world' (21 February 1996). Sherlockians also produce pastiches, both serious and parodic, that attempt to replicate Watson/Doyle's style and plotting, but I will not deal with this aspect of fan writing here. Rather I wish to investigate the ways in which the Hounds of the Internet resort to historical arguments in their discussions of the Holmesian canon.

First, however, who are the Hounds and what do they generally talk about? Let us begin with a geographic profile. As of February 1996, 475 users subscribed to the list-server, the majority of these, 401, having e-mail addresses in the US, a number consistent with the greater penetration of the Internet in that country.[12] The other users resided in the following countries: Argentina, 1; Australia, 6; Brazil, 2; Canada, 25; Denmark, 3; France, 1; Germany, 1; Great Britain, 16; India, 1; Ireland, 2; Israel, 1; Italy, 1; Japan, 6; Malta, 1; Netherlands, 1; New Zealand, 1; South Africa, 2; and Sweden, 3. Without actually having counted, my impression is that postings to the bulletin board come primarily from the US, Canada and Britain, as might be expected given the geographic distribution.

Although I do not subscribe to the truism that entering cyberspace frees one from all demographic determinants, I do admit that, without extensive analysis of actual postings, it is extremely difficult to determine such characteristics as the race and class of the bulletin board users. However, one can safely assume that the Hounds, like most Internet users, are predominantly white and middle-class. I have done a rough calculation of the Hounds' gender: 284 men, 124 women (including the author) and 67 posters whose gender I cannot identify.[13] These numbers are consistent with figures concerning the gendered use of the Internet, but even splitting the unknowns evenly between men and women results in 317 men and 157 women, or 67 per cent male and 33 per cent female. The frequency of postings by gender conforms to this distribution. Of the 81 postings that form the data for this article, 35 per cent originated from women.[14]

More important than these admittedly crude demographics is the following categorisation of the most frequently discussed topics, which is, I admit, impressionistic rather than statistical and is listed in no particular order of frequency:

1) Sherlockian scholarship of both the serious and the parodic kind; Conan Doyle scholarship.
2) 'Psycho-biographical' speculations about the characters – why did Holmes never marry? What was the relationship between Holmes and Watson?
3) Pastiches posted to the list.
4) Comments about screen versions of the canon and the actors portraying the characters.
5) Personal connections to the canon – a relative named John Watson, for instance, or considerations of why Holmes might be an attractive romantic partner.
6) Trivia questions.
7) 'Real' community maintenance – announcements of events or reports of scion societies.
8) 'Virtual' community maintenance – routine subscribe and unsubscribe messages as well as more personal messages – 'I've been sick but now I'm back'.
9) Discussions of related fictional characters.
10) Sherlockian commodities – 'I have this for sale'; 'Where can I purchase this?'
11) Computer queries – where to find Sherlockian information on the World Wide Web.
12) Reviews of recently released films, television programmes, books, and so forth.

Sherlockians in cyberspace, then, most likely roughly conform to the demographic profile of other Internet fan groups and seem to discuss much the same topics. But unlike cyberspace Trekkies and the fans of other media products such as soap operas, they make frequent references to a 'real' historical past in their discussions.[15] Let us begin this discussion of the historiographic assumptions and historical experience of the Hounds through reference to other computerised representations of history.

Many text-based computer games, including Adventure, the progenitor of them all that gave rise to the now ubiquitous MUDs, are set in a mythical, that is eternally static, rather than a historical, that is evolving and changing, past. Players in games of this type enter lands that derive characters and plots from fairy tales and legends – magicians, dragons, searches for hidden treasures and rescues of imperilled princesses. Even the most popular of home video games, such as Super Mario Brothers, are simply variants on ancient quest narratives.[16] More 'sophisticated' CD-ROM games, such as Civilisation or SimCity, are seemingly predicated upon the historical, upon evolution and change, as players attempt to lead their virtual charges from nomadic tribes to city states or from small town to thriving metropolis. But the historical here remains at a high level of abstraction: leading the 'Babylonians' does not require detailed knowledge of Babylonian history while your particular SimCity could in fact be any city, or at least any American, city.

Sherlockians on the Internet, indeed Sherlockians generally, maintain a complex, and sometimes contradictory, balance between the mythical and the historical. The Holmes stories appeal to many Sherlockians precisely because of their setting in a bygone age that seems in many respects preferable to their own. Consider some key lines from the sonnet '221B', penned by Vincent Starrett, one of the founding Baker Street Irregulars, during the darkest days of the Second World War when it seemed as if Holmes' England might succumb to the Nazi dreadnought:

> Here dwell together still two men of note
> Who never lived and so can never die:
> How very near they seem, yet how remote
> That age before the world went all awry ...
> Here, though the world explode, these two survive,
> And it is always eighteen ninety five.[17]

The sonnet's last line provides a Sherlockian rallying cry and the title for this article, as well as the foundational principle for the game of Sherlockian scholarship the Hounds of the Internet play. Contributing to a thread concerning the proper form of address for widows, 'John Scott Eccles' wrote: 'As a new contributor, I assumed that the Hounds work on the basic Holmesian premise that it "is always 1895" and I was describing the proper usage that was current in this country (i.e. the United Kingdom of Great Britain and Northern Ireland) towards the end of the reign of Her late Majesty Queen Victoria' (29 February 1996).

The stories' settings of gaslights, hansom cabs and pea soupers are as mythical to denizens of the late twentieth century as dragons' caves and enchanted castles, while Holmes himself functions as a legendary hero of sorts, setting right wrongs that resist the intervention of mere mortals. Many commentators on the so-called 'classical' detective story, which includes Conan Doyle as well as practitioners of the country-house mystery such as Agatha Christie, have noted that the detective serves as the guardian of the status quo by defeating a villain associated with the forces of disruption. Professor James Moriarty is, of course, the archetypal villain and some commentators as well as writers of pastiches, have drawn a connection between the great detective and his nemesis, speculating that he represents an out-of-control and antisocial Holmes. Despite his bohemian tendencies, however, Holmes adhered to and employed in his work a nineteenth-century scientific rationalism, descended from the Enlightenment, whose proponents' limitless optimism believed that such an epistemology could be employed only for good. Having found vampires in his commonplace book, Holmes commented, 'Are we to give serious attention to such things? This agency stands flat-footed upon the ground, and there it must remain. The world is big enough for us. No ghosts need apply.'[18] The horrors of a world war and the loss of a son had driven his creator to seek solace in spiritualism, but Holmes still firmly rejected the paranormal in favour of the 'world'. But in our post-Enlightenment, postmodern world, such faith in scientific rationalism seems touchingly old-fashioned. In the late twentieth century, ghosts may not only apply but are often provided with gainful employment, as witness the phenomenal success of *The X Files* and other mass media products of a supernatural nature.

In our millennial era, the appropriation of Holmes as a hero of nineteenth-century rationalism may be motivated by a longing for a mythic and reassuring age, albeit one that has little relevance for contemporary life except by contrast. I want to go further by suggesting that a 'virtual community' may be the perfect forum for such an appropriation. Like Howard Rheingold, many 'blue skies' commentators on the 'information superhighway' extol its potential for rebuilding community in a world where community no longer exists. Kevin Robins, however, takes a refreshingly sceptical view. 'You might think of cyberspace as a utopian vision for postmodern times. Utopia is nowhere and at the same time it is also somewhere good. Cyberspace is projected as the same kind of nowhere somewhere.'[19] Some pages later, drawing an analogy between Disneyland and the Internet, Robins suggests that those seeking community in cyberspace have the desire to 'control exposure and to create security and order ... Cyberspace and virtual reality have seemed to offer some kind of technological fix for a world gone wrong, promising the restoration of a sense of community and communitarian order'.[20] One can hear echoes of the Starrett lines: 'Here, though the world explode, these two survive,/ And it is always eighteen ninety five.' The commonalities between the utopian reassurance provided by an Internet bulletin board service and by the mythical study at 221B Baker Street might make 1895 and Windows 95 more akin to each other than one might initially suppose.

This discussion of the mythic aspects of Sherlockian appropriation on the Internet does not, however, exhaust the contradictory and complex relationship of the Hounds of the Internet to historiography and the experience of history. Robins also comments that 'the technological imaginary is driven by the fantasy of rational mastery of humans over nature and their own nature'.[21] Or, as Holmes said, 'The world is big enough for us', the subtext here being that he and Watson, as late nineteenth-century upper-middle-class white men privileged to live at the hub of Empire exercised mastery over the social and the natural world. For Holmes, technology, science and rapid access to copious information were the foundations of this mastery. Holmes and his creator lived in the period which saw criminal detection evolve from a haphazard system predicated largely upon luck and informants to a methodical science that employed the new techniques of chemical analysis, the mugshot and the forerunner of the fingerprint, the Bertillon system of bodily measurements. As Holmes said to Watson, chiding him for the romantic tone of his stories, 'Detection is, or ought to be, an exact science, and should be treated in the same cold and unemotional manner. You have attempted to tinge it with romanticism, which produces much the same effect as if you worked a love-story or an elopement into the fifth proposition of Euclid.'[22] Even lacking Holmes' native brilliance, one could amass facts, apply logical principles of deduction, and solve any puzzle, no matter how baffling. 'You know my method. It is founded upon the observation of trifles', said Holmes, urging Watson to engage in his own deductions.[23]

Sherlockians pride themselves on following the Master's methods, not only as they attempt to solve his cases along with him, but as they play at the game of Sherlockian scholarship, attempting to impose a coherence upon stories written hurriedly and out of chronological sequence. The amassing of facts concerning the Victorian period aids in both tasks. Take, for example, the thorny question of Watson's wound. During his service as an Army doctor in the Second Afghan War, Watson was wounded by a jezail bullet. But precisely where? With maddening inconsistency the good doctor sometimes speaks of a wound in the shoulder and sometimes of a wound in the leg. Discovering that Afghan snipers often hid on rocky ledges and that Watson may thus have been shot from above enables one to plot a bullet trajectory that could have traversed both his shoulder and his leg.

As I suggested at the outset of this article, computers and the Internet constitute the modern equivalent of Holmes' commonplace books, enabling immediate access to massive compendiums of facts. But such reliance upon facts has implications for the Hounds' historiographic assumptions. Many of the Hounds of the Internet implicitly accept a

nineteenth-century scientific rational/conventional historiography. Like a detective, the hardworking historian needs to
compile and analyse facts, in his case using them to recover
and reconstruct an objective past that constitutes history 'as
it really was', in von Ranke's words. In keeping with this historiographic epistemology, the majority of the Hounds'
historical discussions consist of recitations of facts, references
to 'accepted' historical sources and requests for further
information – more facts and more sources.

Consider the following extract from the daily interchanges
on the Hounds list-server, taken from a thread about the
British army in the nineteenth century:

> Lord Raglan was the overall British commander in the
> Crimea, while the Earls Lucan and Cardigan were the feuding
> brothers-in-law. Major General Lord Lucan, commander of
> the Cavalry Division, of which the Light Brigade was a part,
> was blamed for the misinterpretation of Lord Raglan's order,
> that sent Brigadier Lord Cardigan and his Light Brigade
> charging into the valley ... When the others came home and
> told of the confusion, the losses, and the folly of it all,
> Cardigan became a figure of public mockery. However, the
> heroism of the individual cavalrymen in that battle, is still
> a very proud moment in British history. ('The Persian
> Slipper', 4 March 1996)[24]

The poster relays information to his fellow Sherlockians
through the cutting-edge technology of computer mediated
communication, but the version of the past that he constructs
is the historiographical counterpart to Holmes' commonplace
books, with their records of old cases and accumulated
information. In other words, 'The Persian Slipper' conceives
of history as facts, and primarily facts about 'great men', be
they army commanders or heroic soldiers. This fact-driven
history initially seems at odds with a mythic appropriation of
Holmes, but the poster manages to reconcile conventional
historiography with mythic reassurance by providing an
interpretation of the 'facts'. The Charge of the Light Brigade
may have been a grand military cock-up but we (that is, white
males of British descent or affiliation) can still take pride in

an individual heroism that he seems to imply represents the best aspects of Victorian imperialism. The 'Persian Slipper's interest in Holmes and in history is strongly past-oriented: beyond the reflected glory that we may enjoy from historical events, they have little resonance with the present or the future. A history which remains eternal and unchanging, and which has little or no implications for the present has become myth.

Contrast the 'Persian Slipper's posting with another taken from a thread concerning the economic position of women in Victorian times:

> I was quite aware of the fact that ['A Case of Identity'] involved a woman living at home, but I have also read other sources where respectable women NOT living at home (i.e., shop girls, etc., who lived in boarding houses b/c their families lived in the country) were making about that amount and trying to live on it, too, so the 60 pound/yr figure is not simply for women living at home. Yes, I, too, deplore the 'female tax'. It is more expensive to be female in any age (not just the 20th century), and the thought that I might be paid EVEN LESS is appalling, to say the *least*!! ('Edith Presbury', 27 February 1996)
> (whose grandmother lost her job when she got married, b/c it was illegal for a married woman to teach, regardless of her age or whether or not she ever had children, and whose great-aunt faced the same problem.)

As does 'The Persian Slipper', 'Edith Presbury' dispenses factual information, gleaned from 'other sources', to her fellow Hounds of the Internet: many women survived on £60 a year. There the similarity between the two posts ends. The further 'facts' that the poster conveys come not from traditional historical 'sources', but from her family's oral history. And while 'Edith Presbury' also provides an interpretation of the 'facts', in her case the link that she forges between the annual income figure and the ongoing oppression of women has present-day resonance with her own experiences and those of other women: 'It is more expensive to be female in any age.' Implicit in this sentiment may be a future-orientation: such inequality should not continue. The linking of such discriminatory attitudes to the Victorians reveals their inappropriateness for the late twentieth century.

'Edith Presbury's historiographic approach is the antithesis of 'The Persian Slipper's. On the basis of his post, he might be characterised as an adherent of traditional, narrative history. He accumulates 'facts' from authoritative sources, is concerned with the exploits of 'great men' and keeps his history firmly in the past. On the basis of her post, she might be characterised as an adherent of the new social history that has revolutionised the academy within the past three decades or so. Some of her 'facts' come from the non-traditional source of oral history, she is concerned with the everyday lives of ordinary people and her history resonates with the present and the future, in keeping with many social historians' contemporary political commitments. In short, 'Edith Presbury' engages in a historical rather than a mythic appropriation of Holmes.

These two postings reveal a striking difference between the two Hounds' appropriation of the same popular hero. Yet while the 'Persian Slipper's and 'Edith Presbury's historiography may differ markedly, I want to conclude by suggesting that their involvement in the Hounds of the Internet may affect their experience of history in similar fashion. Here we tread on speculative ground, entailing consideration of those effects of computers upon everyday lived experience that might be hard to articulate within available language structures. A Sherlockian going on-line may find a qualitative as well as a quantitative difference in terms of her interactions with fellow fans and thus in terms of her experience of history. Avid Sherlockians who live in densely populated areas, such as the north-eastern United States, can attend scion society meetings practically on a weekly basis, and, failing this, certainly have informal contacts with other Sherlockians who form part of their friendship network. A subscription to the Hounds list-server brings with it the potential for daily, indeed practically constant, virtual contact with one's fellow fans, who devote a great deal of their time to the discussion of Victorian history. Even for the 'Persian Slipper', and the other Hounds who engage in a mythic appropriation of Holmes, the past in this sense is no longer cordoned off from the present and future.

For the Hounds, and perhaps for others who discuss history on the Internet, there may be a postmodern blurring of boundaries between past, present and future, as history becomes a less objective, less fixed entity, an ongoing practice that structures the experience of both the present and the future. The technology which facilitates this everyday experience is represented as having the potential to become ever more powerful, promising an ever greater immersion in a past made more and more tangible through computer wizardry. Sherlockians must view with envy, but perhaps also with a certain amount of anticipation, those episodes of *Star Trek: The Next Generation* in which Data and Geordi recreate Victorian London, Holmes and Moriarty on the Enterprise holodeck. When we too can enter that holodeck the past will truly have become present and our prosthetic memories, even though still not literally implanted in our 'wetware', hard to distinguish from 'the real'.

Notes

1. A. Conan Doyle, *The Complete Sherlock Holmes* (Garden City, NY: Garden City Publishing Company, 1938), p. 1219.
2. A few definitions are perhaps in order for the non-computer literate. Computer mediated communication, or CMC for short, entails several categories: e-mail – one to one correspondence; bulletin board services, known as BBSs, which entail posting to a central server and the dissemination of posts to all the subscribers; and usenet – the 'chat' groups now often accessed through Web browsers such as Netscape. Also important to networked Sherlockians are the various Holmes homepages on the World Wide Web. I shall discuss these in the larger project of which this article is a component but will not have space to discuss it here.
3. Tony Bennett and Janet Woollacott, *Bond and Beyond: The Political Career of a Popular Hero* (London: Macmillan, 1987) and Roberta E. Pearson and William Uricchio (eds), *The Many Lives of the Batman: Critical Approaches to a Superhero and His Media* (New York: Routledge, 1991).

4. Deborah Lupton, 'The embodied computer/user', in Mike Featherstone and Roger Burrows (eds), *Cyberspace, Cyberbodies, Cyberpunk: Cultures of Technological Embodiment* (London: Sage, 1995), p. 99.

5. Harold Rheingold, *The Virtual Community: Homesteading on the Electronic Frontier* (Reading, MA: Addison-Wesley, 1993), p. 6.

6. Steven G. Jones (ed.), *Cybersociety: Computer-Mediated Communication and Community* (Thousand Oaks: Sage, 1995).

7. Alison Landsberg, 'Prosthetic memory: *Total Recall* and *Blade Runner*', in Featherstone and Burrows, *Cyberspace*, p. 175.

8. See, for example, Camille Bacon-Smith, *Enterprising Women: Television Fandom and the Creation of Popular Myth* (Philadelphia: University of Pennsylvania Press, 1992) and Henry Jenkins, *Textual Poachers: Television Fans and Participatory Culture* (New York: Routledge, 1992).

9. See, for example, John A. Hodgson (ed.), *Sherlock Holmes: The Major Stories with Contemporary Critical Essays* (New York: St Martin's Press, 1994).

10. The fact that no one company holds copyright to the Sherlock Holmes novels/stories is certainly a factor.

11. I should note that many of my friends within the Sherlockian world would contest the appellations of 'fan' and 'fandom', their resistance to these labels stemming from an implicit hierarchisation of the print media over the moving image media. Were this an 'ethnographic' study of the kind undertaken by Jenkins or Bacon-Smith, this viewpoint would be more fully articulated within this article. I should also note that I am myself a 'lapsed' Sherlockian, who for many years participated in Holmes fandom and count many of my best friends among those whom I met in Sherlockian circles.

12. To join the Hounds of the Internet send a subscribe message to listserv@listserv.kent.edu saying 'subscribe hounds-l [your full name]'. To send messages to the list itself the URL is hounds-l@listserv.kent.edu

13. This calculation is hampered by several factors. Some posters use initials and some use pseudonyms. Some

foreign names are not readily assigned to a gender. Some posters might be listed twice at different addresses. Posters are not obligated to use their 'real names'. And some posters may be using partners' or friends' accounts.

14. Again, these are very rough figures. Many of the 81 postings concerned the place of women in Victorian society or Victorian sexuality, topics which may have elicited more interest from the female Hounds. It is also not possible to determine, without longer monitoring and more number crunching than I care to do, how many of these postings come from 'regulars' and how many from occasional 'drop-ins'.

15. It would be interesting in this regard to compare the Hounds to discussion groups devoted to other well-known authors and fictional characters from the past such as, for example, Jane Austen.

16. Mary Fuller and Henry Jenkins, 'Nintendo© and new world travel writing: a dialogue', in Jones, *Cybersociety*, pp. 57–72.

17. Vincent Starrett, '221B', in Edgar W. Smith (ed.), *Profile by Gaslight: An Irregular Reader About the Private Life of Sherlock Holmes* (New York: Simon and Schuster, 1944), p. 290.

18. Doyle, *The Complete Sherlock Holmes*, p. 1219.

19. Kevin Robins, 'Cyberspace and the world we live in', in Featherstone and Burrows, *Cyberspace*, p. 135.

20. Ibid., p. 152.

21. Ibid., p. 137.

22. Doyle, *The Complete Sherlock Holmes*, p. 92.

23. Ibid., p. 240.

24. I admit to some confusion as to the proper citation form for an e-mail communication, a confusion compounded by the fact that I have been 'lurking' on the BBS without revealing my gathering of data for this article. Since the private or public status of these BBS communications is probably subject to legal debate and I have neither informed my subjects of my study nor asked their permission to quote their posts, I have decided to provide only Sherlockian pseudonyms, not names as they appear in e-mail addresses.

Index